DESIGN
MIXOLOGY

DESIGN MIXOLOGY

THE INTERIORS OF TINEKE TRIGGS

CHASE REYNOLDS EWALD

HEATHER SANDY HEBERT

Gibbs Smith

CONTENTS

FOREWORD 7

INTRODUCTION 9

CITY LIVING 13

BEAUTY AND THE BEAST 15

BOLD AND BALANCED 27

TEXTURAL TREASURES 39

URBAN ECLECTIC 51

FASHION FORWARD 63

GREEN WITH ENVY 79

FURTHER AFIELD 88

ALL ABOUT MARILYN 91

TRADITIONAL TWIST 107

MAVERICK ROMANCE 121

BAYFRONT DEBONAIRE 137

GLAM GETAWAYS 147

MOUNTAIN MODERN 149

CAMP GETAWAY 159

A PLACE TO PLAY 171

SURF SCENE 183

PARTY WAVE 195

COASTAL CABANA 205

DESIGNER SHOWCASE 216

DAVID AND IMAN 219

EN VOGUE SALON 225

LIQUID LOUNGE 231

PROJECT TEAMS 236

ABOUT THE AUTHORS 238

ACKNOWLEDGMENTS 239

FOREWORD

BY ERINN VALENCICH

Sometimes you just know. Some people you instantly fall for. Tineke Triggs is one of those people to me. I recall climbing the stairs to her San Francisco office to meet her for the first time. She was a good client of my furniture brand, ERINN V., and I was excited to finally meet her as I had heard so many good things from my team and around our showroom, Hewn.

In the design world, we are all driven by creative pursuits and by our desire to make the lives of others more beautiful by the art we create and weave into living, breathing environments—within which stories unfold. Yet some designers are also keen businesspeople. These are the rare beasts. These are the ones who are eminently passionate about designing every detail of a thing, a space, a home, a landscape—but can also spreadsheet their faces off, manage complex teams, juggle budgets and timelines and client management, and still get home in time to have a full family life. This is Tineke.

I fell for her instantly. Her work is gorgeous, as anyone can see, but if you meet her and spend time with her, you'll instantly fall for her too. She has helped me, inspired me—and many others—with her wit, her charm, her good taste, but most importantly, her kind heart, sharp mind, and genuine character. There is no pretense with Tineke or her work. It's honest, and she's honest. A rare quality that I value and admire.

I hope you enjoy the glimpse into her life and her art. She's truly a one-of-a-kind friend and consummate professional. I aspire to run my businesses as she does hers, and I always look forward to cocktails and conversation with this wonderful woman I get to call my friend.

INTRODUCTION

BY TINEKE TRIGGS

I'm often asked what drives me, what inspires my creativity, and what pushes me to come up with new ideas, engage new clients, and take on new challenges. My answers are hunger, confidence, passion, and empathy. Feelings are the beating heart of every design—I love what I do. The design world is always changing, I'm constantly learning—and I will never, ever get tired of it.

My story isn't a traditional interior designer's story. My path to interior design wasn't straight or obvious, but as a self-taught designer, I've absorbed the influences I've gained along each step of my circuitous route. Through my journey, I've not only gathered knowledge but also developed grit and a great deal of creative confidence.

I've always been hungry for knowledge and information, wanting to feed my creativity by discovering what is around the next corner. I'm the daughter of immigrants who moved to the United States to find a better life. My dad came to the United States from Holland, and my mom is from Scotland. Although I was born and raised in Northern California, I've always felt a connection to Europe. I grew up in a modest household, moved around a lot in my childhood, and pushed through undiagnosed dyslexia throughout my school career.

Early on, I buried myself in drawing, painting, and sketching. It was calming, and it offered an escape from other difficulties in my life. I would draw constantly, my notebooks filled with landscapes, churches, and bridges. We didn't travel much—I was twenty-one when I boarded my first airplane—so most of my creativity came from within my head. Then I started to win art contests—a national Kellogg's illustration contest in fifth grade and another national contest for 7UP in junior high school. Drawing helped me build confidence in my ability to be creative.

I was the first in my family to attend college, majoring in math at UC Santa Barbara. I took art classes but didn't yet know I could build a career in design, and I definitely didn't think I could support myself as an artist (being a starving artist was not part of my plan). I also discovered that I loved to connect with people. I started to travel, taking my first trip to Mexico, then spending a summer in Europe and, after graduation, traveling for a year by myself in the South Pacific and Southeast Asia.

I lived in Chicago, and for my thirtieth birthday, I hiked and biked my way through Kenya, which was a dream trip. I worked in investment banking and sales, developing a background in project management and systems that would eventually serve me well. I was successful but hadn't even registered the possibility that I could have a career I was passionate about. However, I was gathering the tools I needed, even if I wasn't aware of it at the time.

After seven years and a move back to California, I had enough money to buy a place. (In San Francisco, believe it or not!) But I only had the money to buy it, nothing more, and it needed much more. Then something magical happened. My neighbors—a fantastic couple with construction and real estate backgrounds—took me under their wing and taught me to do everything myself. I added stainless steel to an old refrigerator and crown moldings; I even designed and built railings. I developed the knowledge of construction and craft that would become one of my strengths.

I realized that design was just another canvas, and that my ability to draw in two dimensions was out there in three dimensions. I wanted to learn more. I renovated and flipped several apartments, and better yet, I started to find my own voice. Then I took the leap and quit my job. I told myself I'd give it five years.

I'm self-taught, and I've learned from every experience I've had along the way. I'm fearless in my approach to design, but as much as I like to take risks, ultimately, my design approach is also timeless. I always ask myself what the house needs and try to explore its unique history and the pragmatic variables of the structure. I grew up with things that were handed down, so I love when things that have a little bit of history. We all have stories, and our homes hold those stories. I weave my clients' histories and stories into their homes. Everything is connected, and you can follow the lines of my clients' stories as you walk through their homes.

The root of our design process is empathy and building connections. We take the time to get to know our clients in a deep and meaningful way. We ask about color and texture and what they like and dislike. But we also ask about their family history, where they grew up, and where they've traveled. What is the feeling they want their house to have? What is the personality they want to come through? That way, we can design a home that tells their story. It takes time, but it never fails. We become part of their story—like a character actor in their play. We're confident enough to trust each other's instincts, and then it really gets fun.

I'll never forget what one of my clients told me after visiting one of my showcases: "We've been holding you back!" And their advice to one of my later clients: "Just let her go!"

It's one thing to be a good designer. It's another thing to be a good boss. Design does not happen in a silo, and no one does this alone—I have a fantastic team. For over twenty years, I've worked to develop the processes, systems, and communications that let us all be the best we can be. Last year my team and I celebrated twenty years of design practice. I have seldom taken a step back in those two decades to truly appreciate and celebrate our accomplishments. This book gives me a chance to do that.

This book—and my design practice—are a passion project, and now I get to share them with you.

CITY LIVING

BEAUTY AND THE BEAST

The epitome of cool, this San Francisco home is edgy, dramatic, and inviting, all at the same time. To truly appreciate this house, it's important to dive beneath the surface of things because this home is all about the narrative—a story that is unique to this couple and the way they want to live.

Scott Taylor, a VP of video game development at Zynga, and his wife, Kristine Boyden, a public relations executive, weren't looking to move. In fact, they had just renovated a condo nearby when this house—an 1870s San Francisco Edwardian—came on the market. One of the original houses in the city's Mission District, it is buffered by rare side yards and a spacious backyard. Vibrant and full of life, the neighborhood suited the couple perfectly, so they snapped it up, knowing it was where they wanted to put down roots.

For Tineke, design is about divining the true story of the characters who will play out their lives in the homes she designs. She started with a clean slate, then took a deep dive to discover how these clients lived their lives. She found that theirs is a story of city boy meets farm girl—Scott leans toward the wild, while Kristine modulates by holding out for practicality and elegance.

The exterior remains the same to maintain the home's sense of history. To step inside is to become part of a wildly creative story, a bit like a make-believe game of *Dungeons and Dragons*. The juxtaposition between exterior and interior forms a creative tension that gives the design its magic. The magic also derives from a united team, with the clients, Tineke, architect Ari Gessler, and contractor Aaron Gordon all working together in the same direction, developing the type of trust that allows creativity to run free.

Scott and Kristine compare the relationship to a musical group so in tune that they can jam together, riffing off one another to create something extraordinary. "It formed a space for us all to be creative, where we could have these crazy ideas, and Tineke, Ari, and Aaron could just run with them," says Scott.

Themes of art as storytelling, creative juxtaposition, and personal narrative carry through every element of the design. On the main floor, sensuous furnishings and dark hues balance traditional white moldings. In deliberate contrast, a monolithic steel fireplace surround is dropped into the traditional dining room. Custom bookcases slide aside to reveal a hidden door, a clever solution that provides access to the powder room and—in an unexpected twist—Daniel Goldstein's artwork "Invisible Man."

In the sizeable adjacent kitchen, a farmhouse sink, limestone and zinc counters, and bar stools that swing out from the central island give a nod to the home's history and Kristine's country childhood, while the deep gray hue of the cabinets ensures that the kitchen maintains a cool sophistication.

"I LOVE UNIQUE, EDGY DESIGNS. THIS MIGHT BE THE MOST FUN I'VE EVER HAD ON A PROJECT."

The narrative continues in the more private spaces upstairs. In the master bedroom, a Gothic-style bed (custom-designed by Tineke), along with the sinuous lines of an animistic chair, gilded bedside tables, and walls covered in deep blue textured wallpaper, create a moody yet soothing retreat. In the master bath, a symphony of textures plays out in black and white—the rippling waves of the custom-designed vanity, the striations of the shower's white tiles, the dark floors in a herringbone pattern.

Far below, a new underground man cave carved out below the house provides space for Scott to pursue his passions for music and technology. The couple calls it the "cave of entropy." In a play on the narrative of darkness and corruption, a sculptural artwork resembling a tentacled monster (invented by Scott's favorite science-fiction writer H. P. Lovecraft) snakes its way out of the studio, struggling to break free from its subterranean lair but stopping just short of the spiral stair, not quite able to reach the upper floors. Except when it does…emerging subtly in the shiny, black tiles that cover the walls of the powder room on the home's main floor, a tamed version of the dark presence bubbling up from below.

Every narrative needs a good plot twist.

Previous overleaf: The sweeping spiral stair, the core building element around which all else revolves, was custom-designed to encircle "Diver," by artist Daniel Goldstein, which cascades down the stairwell like a crown jewel.

Opposite: The couple, avid supporters of local artists, has curated a collection that is like a thread of community weaving through the home. In the small living room just off the dining room, Tineke assembled sculptural furniture to complement a Kate Nichols painting and a plaster skull from turn-of-the-century Paris. The Magnolia Pod Coffee Table by Avrett, with its subtle thorns, is just a little bit dangerous, and the custom velour sofa is intricately stitched to resemble a woven herringbone.

Above: In the large kitchen, a La Cornue stove, tiled backsplash by Ann Sacks, and unlacquered brass faucets by Waterworks evoke the building's history. The Synapse pendants by Avrett illustrate a signature Tineke Triggs approach: taking traditional elements and carrying them out in nontraditional ways. Instead of the expected candelabra, the clear globes house a tangle of wires—an explosion of electricity evocatively at odds with the traditional forms.

Opposite top: Shades of pink and purple soften the kitchen's dark grey hues. In typical fashion, Tineke found a wallpaper pattern—Cloud Toile by Timorous Beasties—and saw new potential, translating the design into fabric for the kitchen's Roman shades.

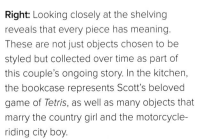

Right: Looking closely at the shelving reveals that every piece has meaning. These are not just objects chosen to be styled but collected over time as part of this couple's ongoing story. In the kitchen, the bookcase represents Scott's beloved game of *Tetris*, as well as many objects that marry the country girl and the motorcycle-riding city boy.

Opposite: Creative tension reigns in the dining room, where a contemporary steel-front fireplace quietly shakes up a room trimmed in traditional moldings painted in all-white. Iconic loop dining chairs from Noir, initially designed by Frances Elkins in the 1930s, are stained black. Wing chairs from Plantation, customized with textural, fringy backs—occupy the places of honor at a custom table of hammered iron and ebonized oak.

Above and right: Bookcases in the dining room slide apart to reveal the entry to the powder room, a creative solution that simultaneously solved a practical challenge and provided an opportunity to dramatically reveal "Invisible Man" by Daniel Goldstein. Composed of hypodermic needles, the artwork is a vivid reference to the spread of AIDS.

Above: The sinuous lines of an animistic chair from Coup D'État provide a striking complement to the Gothic bed and textured wallpaper.
Opposite: Tineke created a gothic vibe with a custom headboard, Bernhardt bedside tables in a patinated brass finish, and embossed vinyl wallpaper with the aspect of an eel skin from Élitis in a color aptly named "Follement Glamour." Sconces are formed from individual candleholders, fused and fitted with LED bulbs resembling lightsabers.

Opposite: Hidden lighting softly washes the walls of the powder room, cloaked in black bubble tile from ANNE SACKS and a Rorschach-like Timorous Beasties wallpaper on the ceiling, all reflected in the off-kilter form of a mirror from Oskar Zieta. Says Tineke, "I almost cried when I found that mirror."

Above left and right: Layers of texture reign in the master bathroom. A custom Tineke Triggs vanity is imbued with a wavelike sense of movement, while a noir candelabra references Gothic candlelight in a modern form. Tineke delights in finding must-have objects and turning them into something new, like the his-and-hers sconces crafted from two decorative hands. "It's all about the unexpected, right?" says Tineke.

Right: Scott has an affinity for multi-legged creatures that, upon close observation, make appearances throughout the home. At her client's request, Tineke recruited San Francisco Opera prop maker Qris Fry to create "Corruption," a stylized interpretation of Cthulhu, a mythical creature invented in 1926 by science fiction writer H. P. Lovecraft.

BOLD AND BALANCED

Every house has its own rhythm.

In the case of this unique project, Tineke created that rhythm by skillfully orchestrating a succession of bold, saturated rooms that alternate with calm, neutral spaces to form a home that exists in perfect harmony with her clients, their personal stories, and the way they live. Tineke knew the clients and the property well, as she had already worked with the family to reenvision their Stinson Beach weekend house. And the house itself? It sits next door to Tineke's own home in San Francisco.

The three-story house was long on potential but short on personality. "I had known this property for close to 20 years. It was a small Edwardian home purchased and flipped by a developer who, sadly, had turned it into a brown box as he tried to capture as much square footage as possible. "When he put it up for sale, I knew it had great potential if you looked past the current layout," says Tineke.

Her clients were looking for a permanent home. A family of five, they had been renting in the Presidio for ten years and wanted to create a place to entertain, with various spaces to suit their family and inspire their creativity. Tineke walked them through the property to help them visualize the possibilities.

They bit. They bought it. Then they gutted it.

What emerged from that visionary move is a contemporary, open floor plan with a symphony of spaces, each with its own personality but connected by a distinct sense of rhythm and purpose. For Tineke, it's these connections that make the design so successful. Grand enough to host extended family gatherings, it is also intimate and highly personal—perfect for this family, who would become her next-door neighbors.

In the dining room, a statement Henge chandelier fixture from Coup D'État hangs above a Hellman Chang dining table, and the walls are covered in Phillip Jeffries wallpaper.

"It had to be done right," says Tineke. "If not, I'd hear about it every day!"

The front room—now the "salon"—is undoubtedly the home's statement room. The clients were looking for a hip vibe, which Tineke delivered in spades, cloaking the room in high-gloss lacquer walls in a deep shade of blue, softened with sweet rose-colored chairs and topped off by a vintage Sputnik chandelier. This piece is Tineke's personal favorite and the first item she purchased for the house.

"I love everything about this room," says Tineke. "The cozy sofas, the lucite table, the vintage chandelier. It's a great mix of traditional and vintage—playful and sophisticated—masculine and feminine."

The elongated room was originally off-kilter. The windows weren't centered, and the room needed balance. In typical fashion, Tineke thought outside the box, adding a moveable bookcase that not only brought balance to the room but opened to reveal a hidden office tucked behind it. Adjacent to the salon, the dining room is more subdued but no less artful—a place the family gathers often. The crane, who came to the home with the family, feels right at home here and has even been known to dress up for holidays.

Every Tineke Triggs project inevitably includes a bit of magic. Off the dining room lies Tineke's favorite room—a hidden powder room tucked behind a wallpapered door set seamlessly into the wall. Draped in blue vinyl wallpaper, the space features vintage light fixtures that Tineke carried all the way from Paris just for this room—truly a labor of love.

The kitchen and living room are like adagios in a dramatic piece of music—the calm between more saturated spaces. Light and airy, the adjacent areas are all about creating a connection between the house and outdoor terrace. The white kitchen is a mixture of old and new, its crisp white cabinetry inset with antiqued mirror and jewel-like pendants suspended over a waterfall island of Calcutta marble. In the living room, an airy palette is an apt transition between the kitchen and the terrace.

Asked about her ability to seamlessly transition from one vocabulary to the next, Tineke responds with a twinkle, "As my husband often says, he's married to many women."

The upper floor holds three of the home's four bedrooms. The emphasis on this level is on creating a serene sanctuary with soft colors and a distinct sense of calm. There is also a bedroom on the ground floor, between the billiard room and the music room, which the couple's teenage daughter immediately claimed as her own.

A trip through the ground floor is an orchestrated journey that gets just a little bit wilder as you progress from the family room to the billiard room to the music room. This collection of spaces—with its eclectic mix of custom and vintage pieces and provocative artwork—speaks to the family's love of music, games, and relaxing together. The culmination of the journey is the recording studio—an homage to the husband's love of vinyl. Hidden behind a leather door and lined with vintage albums, it's completely soundproof so that whatever happens downstairs stays downstairs.

"Everything on the ground floor is warming you up for the recording studio," Tineke says. It's the exclamation point in this home's story.

"I'LL NEVER FORGET THE LOOK ON MY CLIENTS' FACES WHEN I REVEALED THEIR HOME. IT MAKES ALL OF THE HARD WORK WORTH IT. THEY WERE BLOWN AWAY— AND IT WASN'T JUST BECAUSE I GREETED THEM WITH CHAMPAGNE."

Opposite: Tineke often calls lighting "jewelry for the home." The salon's vintage Sputnik chandelier—original provenance in Paris and purchased at Found by Maja—is undoubtedly the home's crown jewel. Rose-hued swivel chairs from HOLLY HUNT and the client's own Lucite coffee table play beautiful supporting roles.

Above: The all-white kitchen is a carefully orchestrated transition where the rhythm of the house slows down. Delicate details—antiqued mirror cabinet doors; graceful, structured pendants from Apparatus; hardware from Design Theory—reinforce the sense of lightness in this part of the house.

Right: A beautiful transitional space, the living/family room is all about connection—to the kitchen on one side and the outdoors on the other. The carpet's mesmerizing pattern of blue and green gently directs the eye toward the outdoors. Everything about this room is inviting.

Top left: A custom wall mural by Elan Evans and bold strokes of royal blue splashed across the shades give this soft pink bedroom a distinct edge.

Left: Tineke believes every room needs a statement piece. In the master bath, it's the floor, covered in Josephine tile custom-designed by Tineke for the Musiek Collection.

Softness reigns in the master bedroom, clothed in blues and grays. Delicate glass pendants hang above clean-lined nightstands, all from HOLLY HUNT. Walls are clothed in soft gray fabric from Phillip Jeffries. "Every bedroom is a sanctuary," maintains Tineke.

"EVERYTHING ON THE GROUND FLOOR IS WARMING YOU UP FOR THE RECORDING STUDIO. IT'S THE EXCLAMATION POINT IN THIS HOME'S STORY."

Opposite: The ground level is a place to play pool, poker, and board games, and it is devoted to the family's love of music. In describing what they were looking for on this level, the husband memorably told Tineke, "We're not Queen—we're the Eagles."

Right: The recording studio is lit by a rotating rainbow of colors from a vintage recording sign—a surprise gift from Tineke to her clients.

TEXTURAL TREASURES

In a family home full of unique details and personal touches, what speaks most to its ethos might be the one-of-a-kind neon signs in each of the daughters' bedrooms. During the process of taking a 1930s Edwardian home from its bland nineties renovation to one reflective of its inhabitants—one full of warmth, interest, and character—Tineke suggested to her clients that the daughters' rooms be personalized. She asked each girl to choose one word that spoke to them and captured their outlook on life or that they aspired to. The results—bespoke neon signs reading "brave," "adventure," and "imagine"—speak not just to the girls but to the home itself.

Tineke's clients brought her on board to address two overriding issues. The architecture of the house had been respected in the update, but the result was devoid of character. In addition, the layout and flow were challenging: too many small spaces, no practical landing place for an active family, and little connection to the outdoors. "They wanted it to be comfortable and welcoming, livable but not oversaturated. I brought in texture to create character and a connection to who these people are as a family."

First, the reconfigurations. Tineke tapped her spatial-awareness superpower to suggest some "brave" moves. She captured some garage space and redesigned the lower floor to create a laundry and mudroom, a TV room, and a guest bedroom. On the third floor, a closet and flue were commandeered to create a more gracious primary suite, with his-and-her walk-in closets and a larger master bath. The biggest transformation was on the main floor. Removing a kitchen wall, partially eliminating a dining room wall, and reorienting the powder room allowed for a kitchen with an island, a breakfast nook, and a family room. The increased openness to the floor plan enhances flow and makes the house feel significantly more spacious.

Above: A 1930s Edwardian was transformed from its bland nineties renovation to one filled with texture and detail. The mandate was to respect the existing architecture while rethinking layout and flow and creating connection to the outdoors. A custom stair railing—elongated rectangles in a dark bronze finish capped with gray-washed oak—makes a lyrical statement that plays through the home's three levels. In the living room, the Entropy Chair by Phillips Collection exemplifies

Tineke's ability to add understated interest to every corner.

Right: The living room was large enough to create two seating areas, one centered on the fireplace, the other a music room. The sofas are covered in Chivasso fabric, the chandelier from Arteriors Home. Unexpected profiles in the Old Studio étagères and Noir Furniture coffee table create small surprises. As for the side chairs, says the designer, "I like pulling in wood to warm up the space."

The bravest move of all? Tineke broke one of her cardinal rules by sacrificing square footage inside the house to create a deck off the kitchen. "Typically in San Francisco homes, when you want to get outdoors you either want to go straight out from the floor that you're on or down one level. But if it's any more than that you're never going to use it," she says. "Normally, you never want to take away square footage in a house, but because I was able to gain in the laundry area, we eliminated a second-level bump out and turned it into a deck. That allowed us to have big French doors to a nice deck off the kitchen and stairs to the backyard. It was one of the few times I broke my rule."

Every house should have some sense of "adventure" that can be found in the clients' statement artwork and photography, unusual lighting, and dramatic tile in the kitchen, baths, and foyer. The homeowners were clear about wanting a neutral palette, so Tineke focused on adding unique textural elements throughout the space: the spiderweb-like Entropy chair from the Philips Collection, covered with a sheepskin, for instance, and a heavily textural wood console and coffee table in the living room. She applied large metal nail heads to the front door to add interest and painted the house a dark charcoal to make it stand out.

The entry tile, an African concrete tile with fun patterns, makes an impact from the moment of entry. In the family room, the fireplace surround runs from floor to ceiling in a bold black geometric tile. "There were lots of elements throughout the house that were consistent but texturally interesting."

Tineke paid homage to the wonders of "imagination" through the many bespoke items created for the home. She designed glass panels and an iron roller track for the open shelving in the kitchen, a rug of her own design in the living room, a chair, bed, dining table, nightstands, and sofas. "I find if I design everything in a box where everything is angular, I struggle to find the interest in a space. I try to pepper in unexpected shapes with the cleaner ones."

The stairway railing might be the home's most impactful feature, and on some level it was the most challenging, she admits. "It was really fun to do this custom-designed staircase; instead of straight pickets, we have these beautiful squares. But you have no idea what a feat it was to get it measured out right; you had to adjust from each angle to figure out exactly how big the squares needed to be to meet code."

The railing design—elongated rectangles in a dark bronze finish, capped with gray-washed oak to match the floors—makes a lyrical statement that plays through and connects the home's three levels. It's elegant and unique, the product of a venerable home, open-minded clients, and unlimited imagination.

"A LOT OF MY GIFTS ARE IN SPATIAL AWARENESS. I FIND IT'S LIKE A PUZZLE, TRYING TO FIGURE OUT HOW TO RECONFIGURE SMALL SPACES AND MAKE THEM MORE USABLE."

Opposite top: Tineke broke her own rule about never taking away square footage in a house to create an indoor/outdoor experience in the kitchen where French doors lead to a deck. The built-in banquette, with neutral upholstery from Christopher Hyland, can accommodate a crowd. The client's black-and-white photographs pair perfectly with the Castor Pendants.

Opposite bottom: The clients were initially hesitant about the impact of the pattern brought by Kelly Wearstler's tile. Now it's one of their favorite features. Tineke designed the glass and iron cabinets in the same materials as the pendants from Roll & Hill. She works hard to find the right lighting fixture: "I like lights to be unexpected and unique."

Above: Tineke worked closely with builder Jeff King to make better use of space on all three levels. On the third floor, the primary bedroom, closets, and bath were reconfigured and space captured from a hall closet and fireplace flue. In the enlarged master bath, Tineke custom-designed the floor tiles. The vanity wall tile is from Global Tile, the lighting fixture from Boyd Lighting. The vanity top is Neolith.

Right: In the tranquil primary bedroom, both the chair and bed were custom-designed by Tineke, the headboard covered with Tiger Leather, the chairs with soft lavender fabric from Pindler & Pindler. The Rejuvenation chandelier and custom rug from Partow Rug contribute to the light and bright feeling of the room. "I love a good four-poster bed. It's quiet and cozy. I like my bedrooms not to be over-saturated but soothing. I wanted it to feel like a hotel." The leather, lacquer, and metal nightstands are custom.

Tineke designed three unique bedrooms for three unique daughters. She worked with each girl on color palettes and created one-of-a-kind neon signs that reflect their personalities. The resulting spaces are full of warmth, interest, and character. The words "brave," "adventure," and "imagine" speak not just to the girls but to the home itself.

URBAN
ECLECTIC

While Tineke loves a good story, she prefers to tell it at her own pace. In a San Francisco home whose exterior presented as stately, inside the house, she says, "There was a lot of meandering through small rooms." While the lack of flow may be typical for the city's Edwardian-period homes, Tineke (working closely with architect Mark Thomas of Hood Thomas Architects and general contractors Jay Blumenfeld and Allison Hammer) believed they could craft a fresh story—one with deliberate pacing, a colorful narrative, and a chronological arc spanning from historical to present day.

The 8,000-square-foot house was replete with views and period details but devoid of many items on the clients' wish list, including a theater, wine cellar, workout room, kids' play area, and connection to the views. (Guest accommodations on the top floor, with two bedrooms, a bathroom, living room, and kitchen, were left intact.) While they agreed on preserving the Edwardian feel, they wanted to contemporize the furnishings as well as the function of rooms like the kitchen and bathrooms.

Equally urgent, in the designer's opinion, was the disconnect between family and furnishings. "The clients were super active; they traveled a ton and were very athletic. But when I looked at the furniture, it felt like old-lady furniture; it just didn't match who they were."

The home has shed that staid image. The exterior reads sophisticated and traditional, while interiors range from bold and moody to light and bright (and in some places, edgy). For this busy family of five, Tineke played with a deft mix of old and new in every room, and with her artful layering of personal items throughout, the house now tells a well-paced story. The narrative starts at the entry with a fearless foray into pattern (Missoni runner on stairs, large-scale graphic rug in the hall) against the black-lacquer stair wall. Pattern is also at play in the living and dining rooms, where blues and whites reference the husband's Swedish heritage. The tone evolves to light and bright in the kitchen with its glassy corner breakfast nook; from there, the family can walk out onto the patio and descend a spiral staircase to the garden.

The lower floor reflects a more carefree attitude, with an open-to-nature playroom complete with a ping-pong table and sky blue built-in display shelves and seating nook, plus cabinets in the same blue with a lively tile backsplash.

On the third floor, family bedrooms reflect their inhabitants. A four-poster bed that had been a family heirloom was turned into a cozy cocoon for one daughter's bedroom. The son's bedroom ceiling features a hand-painted map and the Swedish flag, whose colors are referenced in the furnishings. The primary bedroom is a serene haven, a compact space that seems to double in size when the doors to the deck slide out of sight to reveal a vast sweep of city and bay.

What tells the story of the home, and by extension, the family, most compellingly is the skillful mix of old with new, and Tineke's harnessing of the narrative power of significant objects in spaces throughout the house, most of which reference the family's travels or the homeowner's Swedish heritage. "They like contemporary furnishings, but they had some eclectic pieces," she says, "so what I wanted to do was blend that European traditional vibe with a contemporary one. In the living room, for instance, we created an unconventional bookcase—it almost pops out of the original architecture—to display objects and artworks. And because they'd collected so many things, I created different ways of using those objects throughout the house."

A table from the family's collection, positioned with a mounted cow skull against the black stair wall, was given pride of place in the entry; an old Swedish cabinet was repainted and placed in the dining room. A tapestry purchased by the husband was restored and displayed on a wall, as were vintage bathing suits, flags, a Swedish lock, and African masks. Tineke had a Japanese warrior kimono mounted in an acrylic box to give it a contemporary edge. Says the designer, "They're all such perfect stories."

This expression reaches its apogee in what was once an awkward unused alcove on the landing. Tineke envisioned a library, a place where books could be integral to the family's on-the-go life, whether one sweeps a finger along the spines while racing out the door to a tennis match or interacts with the display by rolling the ladder along the custom-designed track. The space is infused with drama in black lacquer paint, colorful textiles, and an art-piece lighting fixture with hand-blown glass globes. The centerpiece, though, is the leaded stained-glass window designed by Tineke and inspired by Scandinavian quilts.

"In this home," says the designer, "you're feeling the family's history and travel, and the house really communicates that well. And as you're going through the house and experiencing their family and connections, you're getting a peppering of the old and the new. I think that people should live with connections to our past, and this house is the perfect storytelling for that."

A stately Edwardian in San Francisco was given new life for a family of five by Tineke in conjunction with architect Mark Thomas of Hood Thomas Architects and general contractors Jay Blumenfeld and Allison Hammer. "My job," says the designer, "was to make it feel more contemporary, more cohesive, and more connected to the clients' travels, sports, and entertaining." In the living room, Gentry sofa by Moroso, Tiffany chairs by Verdesign, and stools by Gabriel Scott. The custom coffee table was designed by Tineke for a room featuring the Edwardian's original molding. The light fixture is by Moooi.

A sophisticated but playful dining room in which the movement of the custom wool rug from Himalayan Weavers speaks to the drapery fabric, Sultans Suzanni from Martyn Lawrence Bullard. Saarinen chairs from Design Within Reach surround the custom walnut table. The Moooi pendants add a whimsical touch, while the ceiling wallpaper evokes Swedish designs. ERINN V. Diamond Door cabinet in walnut, Alfonso Marina Villiers armoire.

"IT'S THAT OLD AND NEW, THE MORE INDUSTRIAL WITH THE
SOFTER. IF YOU MEET THE CLIENTS, HE'S MORE OF A TINKERER
AND A COLLECTOR—SHE'S MORE WHAT'S FRESH AND NEW.
EVERYBODY'S GOT DIFFERENT STYLES, AND YOU HAVE TO BLEND
THEM SO THE HOME MAKES SENSE FOR BOTH PARTIES."

Above: The light and airy bedroom has pocket doors opening onto its own private deck. The lamps are from Arteriors Home, the bench by Gabby, and the custom Tibetan rug is from The Rug Establishment. The sleigh bed is a family heirloom.

Opposite: One daughter had a collection of Japanese fans, bought for her by her father on his trips to the Far East. Tineke arranged them in an arc over the bed and chose textiles that picked up on their colors and patterns.

Above: In the powder room, whimsical wallpaper puts the visitor in the center of an opera house. The ceiling light is vintage; the light fixtures are from OCHRE. "They are supposed to look like earrings," the designer explains, "but subtle. The lights are quite contemporary, but the mirror is more old-school. Again, it's a play of old and new." **Opposite:** Tineke transformed an unused extra space in the staircase landing into a library complete with rolling ladder. In a nod to the husband's Swedish heritage, a piece of stained glass was replaced with a custom leaded glass design of Tineke's inspired by the patterns in Scandinavian textiles.

FASHION FORWARD

For a classic Spanish Colonial house within a stone's throw of San Francisco's Palace of Fine Arts, the designer had compelling sources of inspiration: the home's Spanish influence, early California references, and the owners' passions and personal history.

"The structure," Tineke explains, "is a beautiful U-shaped home with an inner courtyard. Over the years, it's gone from an original Spanish home to a shabby chic home to an overly complicated traditional home to something so stripped down it was almost too contemporary. When this house came on the market, it was one of those quintessential houses the clients had dreamt about. As a young couple with two kids, they felt like they'd won the lottery."

The charismatic couple are the wife, a fashion executive and designer whose family is Argentinian, and the husband who grew up surfing in a laid-back California coastal town. Both are fashion-forward, family-oriented, and socially active; they planned on entertaining many guests in this ideally located home. These influences gave rise to a narrative arc that links every room in the house through fashion and style references, color, and materiality—leather, iron, plaster—that speaks to Mexico, Spain, Argentina, coastal living, and history. The house and the artwork (which introduce topics as loaded as the role of the Catholic Church in Latin America) are both conversation starters. The furnishings more than do their part to sustain the dialogue.

"I wanted to play into the Latin background, strong women, and fashion undertones while also connecting the husband to his Santa Cruz life. And as I painted the canvas, I wanted to create spaces representing who the clients really are," Tineke explains. "They're beautiful people inside and out who love to entertain. The idea was to create a really fun environment."

Tineke sourced pieces from Spain and Mexico. She made liberal use of leather accents and metal, including hardware from Morocco and Rose Tarlow's hand-forged "The Thorn, the Rose" chandelier, with its Crown of Thorns vibe. And she established consistency with architectural materials, like a limestone table sourced in Paris. "I also brought in tones similar to those you'd see in a Spanish home," she adds, "like rust and mauve-y pinks but in lighter tones."

While Tineke wanted each room to have a connection to the other rooms without being the same. Certain rooms are all about an individual, like the man cave, a mood-saturated space with the feel of an upscale men's club. Tineke exaggerated its lack of height by adding a dark marbled wallpaper on the ceiling to create a den-like coziness. A pool table takes up most of the room; custom bookshelves and liquor bottles displayed on glass shelving keep the focus on hospitality and the life of the mind. A photograph taken in Manhattan, looking up so the skyscrapers form a cross, says Tineke, "ties in the couple's personal history growing up in traditional Catholic families and meeting in New York."

In other places, femininity has its place. "The Vogue Dress," a wire dress made in the shape of an evening gown, is mounted on the wall in one bathroom. In the exuberant powder room, Tineke bejeweled the jungle wildlife herself.

The kitchen was one of the most important spaces in the house, but in an unusual twist, it was almost *too* open. Tineke suggested closing off one of the doors to the sideyard to accommodate a luxe banquette. Open to the kitchen, upholstered in rich green leather, and crowned by a statement chandelier, it grounds the room and plays off the colors in the Moroccan-tiled backsplash. Tineke completed the design with marble countertops and an island with an overhang for casual barstool seating, a place for kids to have breakfast or for guests to perch with a drink.

As one of the primary entertaining spaces, the dining room highlights thought-provoking art, including an Ormond Gigli photograph featuring Ford fashion models in the 1960s and "Truth and Lies," which questions the circumstances surrounding the Brixton riots in the 1980s. "The owners liked the idea of having the art spark the conversation," she explains.

After dinner, guests might discover the speakeasy-like lower level housing a guest bedroom, guest lounge, and a gym. "There," says Tineke, "I decided to embrace the dark and make it sexy. I had artist Elan Evans paint the walls with black and gold lines. The wine cellar and gym have really fun lights. An artist from Mallorca made an art bench that's half wood and lit resin. We made the whole downstairs feel like an art lounge. When people come down for a late-night cocktail, it feels like a moody club."

In the living room of a Spanish Revival home near the Palace of Fine Arts, Tineke combined Verellen sofas, a marble table from Atelier Saint-Jacques, Olivya Stone chairs with HOLLY HUNT fabric, Arteriors Home tables, a handwoven rug from Floor Design, and a Rose Tarlow chandelier. "This is the juxtaposition of light and dark and airy," she says. "I wanted to have a bit of a feminine twist, play off the arches of the Palace, and add contemporary elements but in the same palette as you would see in a traditional Spanish Colonial home. I was going for the more contemporary vibe with the softness of line and interesting shapes to bring it to the current day."

But the house also enjoys the best of town and country. Outdoor dining takes place in a garden designed by landscape architect Topher Delaney, where a classic column imported from Europe plays to the white dome of the 1915 Palace visible over the shrubbery. It is the perfect capstone to a project full of drama, one where the exterior belies an interior that speaks to the architecture while holding all manner of surprises.

"For me, the goal was to capture the youth and beauty of this couple while maintaining the architecture and integrity of the home," says Tineke. "I think that we did a really good job of creating something that represents fashion, uniqueness, and femininity with a stronghold in the masculine and the Spanish while also paying homage to the clients' own cultures and histories. We didn't want anything to feel like it was expected or had been seen. The clients allowed me to take more risks with this project. They wanted it to be a 'Wow!' home, one that truly represented who they are."

Opposite top: Built-in banquette seating upholstered in emerald leather from Tiger Leather makes clever use of an unusually configured space for a breakfast nook. Black leather Casamidy chairs with a black powder-coat finish and a Paul Ferrante chandelier help elevate the casual eat-in dining experience. **Opposite bottom:** In the kitchen, Thomas Hayes Studios chairs add visual interest with their metal crisscross detail and bleached walnut footstools. The colorful and richly detailed tile backsplash speaks to the home's Spanish and Mexican influence. **Above:** Art, objets, color, and tone create a textural palette, Tineke's specialty.

Drenched in autumnal color, upholstered chairs add verve and elegance to the dining room. The black metal frames speak to classic Spanish Colonial materials; the rug from The Rug Establishment was loomed in Arizona. Says Tineke, "The beautiful metal chairs are from DLV, a Spanish manufacturer. The buffet is from Alfonso Marino, also a Spanish manufacturer, and the Gregorius Pineo chandelier is also in that Spanish tradition but with a contemporary twist." Ormond Gigli's iconic image "Girls in the Windows" hangs over the buffet.

Above left: The three-piece brass table is from Olivya Stone. The hand-loomed rug is from Stark. A custom upholstered sofa from S. Harris adds notes of richness and indulgence.

Left: References to fashion and street style abound throughout the house and speak to the couple's passions.

Above: For a couple who loves to entertain, the man cave/pool room gets a lot of use. Covering the ceiling with the Intergalactic wall covering from Chivas was a bold move. It effectively lowers the ceiling, but the result is a cool and moody grown-up space with a club-like vibe, perfect for an after-dinner drink. Custom blue painted woodwork next to open glass bar shelving from Amuneal neatly contrasts tradition with a modern edge. The pool table with black walnut finish is from Crate & Barrel.

"MY GOAL WAS TO LOOK AT THE EXISTING HOME IN ITS ORIGINAL
FORM, WITH ITS BEAUTIFUL PLASTER WALLS AND SPANISH
COURTYARD, AND BRING IN A MORE CONTEMPORARY TWIST
ON THE SPANISH COLONIAL DESIGN WITH A SUBTLE, SEXY
UNDERTONE THAT REPRESENTS WHO THE CLIENTS ARE."

Left: "I love a four-poster bed," says Tineke. This one is in ebonized mahogany from Aesthetic Decor. The array of pieces above the headboard create an ethereal, naturalistic feeling of flow while the fur blanket adds glam. Tineke designed the custom nightstand with leather inlay top in conjunction with Garrett Leather. The chandelier is from Paul Ferrante.

Above: A bedroom vignette shows Tineke's masterful use of tone on tone and includes a custom dresser from Designer Guild in a smoke-like stain finish.

Above: The lower level with lounge, wine cellar, gym, and guest room was envisioned as a kind of speakeasy, a moody-cool destination for after-dinner cocktails. The bed by Verellen was upholstered in oyster with walnut legs and integrated tables. The shams are Chivasso, the handmade Moroccan flooring from Stark.

Right: Lugo lounge chair from Olivya Stone, cognac velvet sofa and marble-top coffee table from CB2. The rug is a custom wool jute-loop knot rug from Tibetana.

Above: The black-and-gold theme continues through the wine cellar and gym door with custom burnished brass hardware from Lowe Hardware.
Opposite: At the stair landing/entry, dramatic black and gold walls hand-painted by artist Elan Evans set the tone for an artsy, edgy experience. Tineke commissioned Tom Price, an artist in Mallorca, to make the wood-and-resin bench, which lights up. The custom rug is Tibetena, the polished brass mirror is from NOVOCASTRIAN.

GREEN WITH ENVY

T im Twerdahl was born and raised in Chicago, spent ten years living in New York City, and considers himself a "city guy" at heart. Although home for Tim, his wife Evita, and his son is in the suburbs south of San Francisco—he wanted a home-away-from-home where they could visit and entertain, and where his son could gain exposure to life in the city. So in 2020, when it felt like nearly everyone was leaving the city for the suburbs or beyond, the family did the opposite.

The home they found, in San Francisco's Pacific Heights neighborhood, is set in a stately 1922 Edwardian home converted into six flats. Lovers of color and art, the couple wanted a place to entertain that was a departure from their more traditional home, so they were ready for color—lots of it. When they saw Tineke's work at the San Francisco Decorator Showcase, they immediately knew her work fit what they were looking for. They told Tineke they were open to being hands off or involved in every detail.

"It turns out I wanted to be involved in every detail," Tim admits with a smile. "And she rolled with that."

The 2,000-square-foot corner unit they purchased had good bones, with lots of light from windows on two sides and pristine period moldings. Painted all white, it was quite literally a blank canvas. To provide an anchor and sense of place as she pushed the interiors in a saturated, contemporary direction, Tineke preserved the period moldings, sometimes keeping them white while drenching the rooms in an interconnected palette of blues, greens, and grays.

The corner living room is the flat's biggest and brightest room. In contrast to the rest of the home, Tineke elected to keep the walls of this room white. "I wanted it to look even bigger," she claims. The colors in this room are drawn from the colors used throughout the house—hues of blue, green, and gray—but here, they are softer, allowing the room to feel washed in light. The result is a breathing space between the flat's more saturated rooms.

Tineke is a master of transition. The view from one room to the next is carefully considered, as is that all-important first glance which is, after all, the first step in an artfully choreographed journey. The view from the living room to the dining room is a perfect example. Seen through a broad opening flanked by a set of graphic artworks, the dining room is masterfully conceived. Deep green walls and dark furnishings are offset with a gilded chandelier and ceiling, contrasting floral and geometric artwork, and the dark rug's kinetic movement—its white-on-black pattern forming the thread that links the light and dark rooms together.

Of course, the view to the office beyond the archway invites investigation. In this room, cloaked in dark gray, a gold screen slides together to mask the computer and other messy necessities that collect in any office. On the wall, the artwork depicts a city street scene, a perfect reference in this urban pied-à-terre.

Though Tim was the most heavily involved in the design process, Evita was passionate

"PEOPLE WANT VIBRANCE AND URBAN EXPOSURE— THEY WANT TO ENGAGE WITH THE URBAN ENVIRONMENT, EVEN IF THEY DON'T LIVE THERE FULL TIME."

about the kitchen. In a reflection of the building's age, the existing kitchen was underutilized. Tineke optimized the L-shaped space by extending it into the adjacent hallway and creating a bar that forms a bridge between the kitchen and dining rooms. The color palette is a sophisticated combination of walnut, satin brass, and cabinets painted a deep blue-gray, with white countertops providing balance. The effect is crisply tailored.

Since this pied-à-terre functions as a getaway, Tineke wanted the bedrooms to feel a little like chic hotel rooms. Restraint and clever use of space maximize the impact of the smaller bedrooms and baths. Dressed in white, green, and pink, the resort-like primary bedroom is like a breath of fresh air, the headboard and smaller, wall-mounted light fixtures providing a nod to hospitality design.

Off the primary bedroom, Tineke took what was once a tiny Jack-and-Jill bathroom and transformed it into an elegant bath. While still small in stature, the room is an impressive study in black and white—light, crisp, and highly functional. Closing in the room's second opening allowed just enough room for a double vanity; a trough sink and wall-mounted faucets save space, and elegant reeded glass allows shared light to flow through the area.

In the living room, Tineke left the existing mantel and painted it all white, adding a marble surround. The Olyvia Stone puzzle table is one of Tineke's favorite pieces.

Top left: The artwork framing the passage from the living room to the dining room is by Sophia Dixon Dillo, whose minimal approach of patterns on a dark ground draws attention to the subtleties of pattern and light.

Left: A peek through the archway leading from the dining room to the adjacent office reveals a custom screen, which slides open for work and closed to hide the mess.

Above: In the dining room, kinetic movement lights up the dark space. A brass Maillon LED chandelier found on 1stDibs contributes glamor, while a rug from the Scott Group introduces a bit of carefully controlled chaos.

The air of hospitality continues in the guest bedroom and the hallway bath. In the guest bedroom—clothed in gray with a pop of complementary orange—small floating nightstands and wall lights invite guests to settle in. In the hallway bath (which does triple duty as the son's bathroom, a guest bath, and powder room), dark gray walls, geometric floors, brass accents, and the energetic movement of Arabescato marble are tightly designed but striking nonetheless.

This pied-à-terre is welcoming, chic, and a little bit fearless, all at the same time. "We are thrilled with how it came out," says Tim. There's no higher praise than that.

Opposite: Appliances and a coffee station are stowed behind fluted glass doors, hidden from view but easily accessible. Pendant lights found in Europe add an unexpected twist.

Above right: The colors and materials of the crisply tailored kitchen fit the room like a perfectly tailored suit.

Right: The new bar—backed with a delicate mosaic tile from Artistic Tile—provides a perfect transition between dining room and kitchen.

Above: In the efficiently designed master bath, reeded glass enclosing the shower and toilet on either side of the vanity allows light to filter through the room. A geometric tile from Artistic Tile is set into a black surround on the floor, and the extreme movement of the Arabescato marble vanity is a feast for the eyes. **Opposite above:** The primary bedroom is a study in green and white with tones of pink. In a stroke of luck, the white stripe separating the two tones of soft green on the Roman shades aligns perfectly with the center mullions on the split-casing windows. **Opposite below:** The guest bedroom and bath deliver a sense of hospitality, cleverly designed to live larger than their actual square footage.

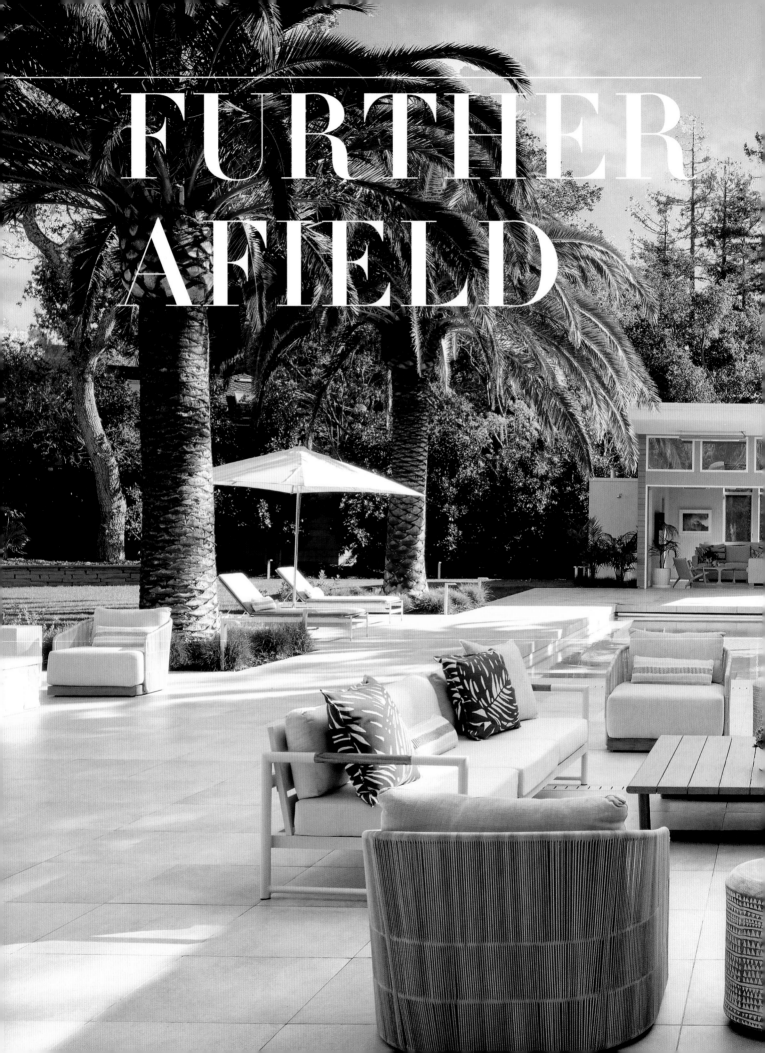

FURTHER AFIELD

ALL ABOUT MARILYN

Jan Byer is a force of nature. It's no accident that her jewelry line—cofounded with a lifelong friend—is named Fierce and Loyal. Raised in the San Francisco Bay Area, she grew up surrounded by fashion as a member of a prominent family with a successful clothing business.

Built in the 1980s, Jan's house is in Southern Marin with beautiful views of the San Francisco Bay. Unfortunately, her house didn't reflect her personality—to put it mildly. "The house was dramatic and interesting, but we needed to bring it forward from the 1980s to today. We changed the palette completely," says Tineke.

"I didn't want a beige house," says Jan. "I wanted something that looked and felt like me."

As she always does, Tineke dove into her client's character. One of the first things she did upon meeting her new client was ask to see her wardrobe, intuiting that Jan's clothing collection would say a lot about who she was and how her surroundings should look and feel. She was right.

Jan is obsessed with Marilyn Monroe. Over the years, she has invested in a valuable collection of artwork and artifacts from Marilyn's life that, until now, remained tucked away in boxes. Not only did Tineke incorporate these artworks and artifacts into the house, but she also used them as her muse. They would become the starting point for themes and color palettes that define the house and its many rooms.

Throughout the house, areas of light and dark, hard and soft, masculine and feminine, form a series of juxtapositions that come together in a distinct and individual sense of rhythm. Varied points of connection—a color, pattern, or detail—subtly stitch the rooms together. It's almost like a game to locate the threads that connect one space to the next, lending a sense of continuity and raison d'être to even the most wildly creative spaces.

"Walking through the rooms of the house is like turning the pages of a good book," says Tineke. "You pick up the story and find the connections. Everything dances together."

The story begins with the dramatic double-height entry. Tineke worked with her favorite decorative painter, Caroline Lizarraga, to create a decorative pink pattern on what were once unadorned white walls. Pink and gilt play a starring role in this house, with an effect that is feminine but not too girly. In a signature play of light and dark Tineke painted the foyer railing stark black, anchoring the space, and installed a statement chandelier that drips down from the ceiling like a piece of statement jewelry.

"Interior design is a lot like putting together a great outfit—mixing a couture bag with off-the-rack jeans, costume jewelry with heirlooms and diamonds. I love to mix high and low, new and vintage, masculine and feminine to create a look that is completely unique," declares Tineke.

The once-dark living room is now light and bright, a quiet space for entertaining friends and enjoying the view. Clothed in white, pink, and gold, there is a sense of Art Deco in the soft curves and fluted fireplace surround that make this room feel fresh and modern.

"There is a Deco revival going on right now that I just love," says Tineke. "It's a good kind of modern for me."

The light-filled foyer and living room transition to a trio of darker rooms—dining room, powder room, and office—creating a pattern that moves from light to dark and back again. Just off the living room lies Jan's favorite room, the office. Tineke calls it the "go for the gusto" room. In this room, there was no holding back: black walls, floor, and furnishings play up the drama, highlighted by the slashes of white in the rug, the curtains, and a sinuous chaise that looks like a female form reclined to take in the view.

Visible from the foyer, the dining room is positively regal, with its dark walls, gilded accents, and lipstick-hued seating. It started, of course, with an iconic painting of Marilyn. "It always starts with Marilyn," Tineke jokes. Actually, it started with her lips. Dining chairs are cloaked in printed pleather to match the lipstick hue, and painted gilt swirls update the original curved ceiling. The banquet, its fluting turned horizontally and inset with brass, forms one of the many threads knitting the rooms together.

Off the dining room, the kitchen, breakfast area, and sitting room transition back to a lighter palette, flowing easily together in a single connected space. Jan spends a lot of time here, so Tineke took care to make it comfortable. A large bouclé sofa is perfect for kicking back and watching television, and two of Jan's favorite Marylin pieces set the tone for the rug and throw pillows. The open kitchen's original cherry cabinets and dark counters have been transformed with an all-white palette, and the breakfast nook is a playful spin on the dining room's glamorous color scheme.

Opposite: The dramatic foyer combines custom tile by Tineke Triggs, painted walls by Caroline Lizarraga, and statement lighting. "Jan loves jewelry and works with it, so she really let me play with the light fixtures," says Tineke.

Opposite: The living room is full of feminine curves. For the floor, Tineke custom-designed a rug, manufactured by the Rug Company, that looks like liquid marble.

Above: "This whole room is about the view and the art," says Tineke. Above the console, an abstract painting by Vicky Barranguet, whose work is inspired by her husband's music, was commissioned specifically for the room.

"I absolutely believe a dark room becomes more expansive," says Tineke of the dark office. The design began with the vintage chairs, which set the tone for the room. On the walls, a custom wood panel wall covering by Philip Jeffries faintly echoes the cerusing on the chairs. On the floor, a white pattern dances with a flourish through the black background of a custom rug by Erik Lindström.

Top left: The custom bar, painted Benjamin Moore's "Black Beauty," is lined in a geometric pattern that plays well with the cabinetry's brass pulls. **Top right:** Tineke is known for her striking powder rooms. Here, a custom-painted reptilian texture adds depth. An asymmetrical mirror and uneven set of light fixtures extend along the longer wall of the small, L-shaped room, their imbalance bringing balance to the space. **Above:** In the dining room, the controlled chaos of gilded swirls updates the original curved ceiling, its brass tones echoed in the chandelier and sconces and inlaid into the sideboard's fluted front.

Jan loves to hang out in the large, open-plan kitchen/breakfast room/family room. Tineke set the new island at a 45-degree angle to improve the flow of the open-plan space. The breakfast room is pulled together like a perfect outfit, with lipstick pink chairs, a black and gold chandelier from Visual Comfort & Co. Signature, and a zebra rug just for fun.

"JAN IS GLAMOROUS WITH AN AIR OF ROCK AND ROLL. MY GOAL FOR HER HOUSE WAS TO MAKE IT HERS AND HERS ALONE."

Upstairs, the private spaces are feminine and serene. The neutral tones of the primary and guest bedrooms create a sense of retreat and play up the importance of texture. The atelier—where Jan works on jewelry, holds meetings, and hosts jewelry clients—is an airy mixture of gold and white, topped by a delicate ceiling pendant that looks like it might have been crafted by a milliner. Tineke and her team worked with a museum curator to craft custom acrylic display boxes for Jan's cherished collection of Marilyn artifacts.

With Tineke by her side, Jan set out to make her expansive Mill Valley house her own. Now the house fits her like a glove. "Now if someone walks into my house," Jan says, "they know it's mine."

Above: Jan's bedroom is a cozy retreat with a wall-to-wall upholstered headboard in a geometric stitch pattern that offsets the soft curves of the love seat and table lamps.

Opposite: The spacious master bath features a soothing mix of curves, Art Deco–inspired geometric forms, and the luxurious movement of marble.

Opposite: In the guest bedroom, an ethereal, cloudlike pattern flows from ceiling to wall, again painted by Caroline Lizzagara. "She is my muse," declares Tineke. "Whatever I can think up, she can paint."

Top right: In the jewelry atelier, three graceful arches line the wall—two housing storage and the third entirely lined in mirror so Jan's clients can try on pieces of her collection.

Bottom right: Every inch of the guest bath, with its beautiful marble and purple walls, recalls a well-tailored outfit. In fact, the vanity, painted in a high gloss and studded with nails, was inspired by the detailing on one of Jan's black leather jackets.

TRADITIONAL TWIST

Tineke has an innate ability to gently encourage her clients to venture outside their comfort zone. For this home just south of San Francisco, that meant working with her clients—an easy-going, family-oriented couple with two teenage children—to create a dynamic environment by gently pushing its traditional vocabulary into new territory.

For this project, a traditional Tudor home that "looked like it had been there for hundreds of years," Tineke worked with architect Eric Nyhus. What began as a limited remodel quickly became a full-scale, down-to-the-studs renovation. While Eric faithfully restored the original exterior architecture—"Good architects can find the history in a house," she says—Tineke embarked on an entirely new approach to the interior.

Through their previous collaborations, Tineke knew this couple loved color and pattern, leaning toward reds, oranges, and blues. For their new home, she encouraged them to experiment with an expanded palette and a more contemporary use of pattern to amp up the eclectic aesthetic. When Tineke suggested painting the entire living area in a single shade of blue—a bold, project-defining statement that nudged the space's traditional detailing in a distinctly modern direction—the clients embraced the decision. The sleek lines of the contemporary fireplace underscore the subtle juxtaposition.

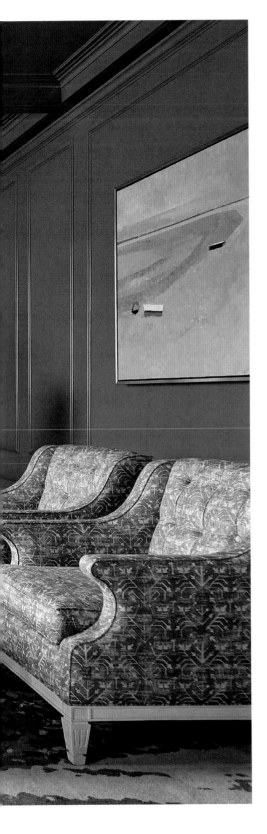

Left: The living room is artfully arranged with the lighter chairs near the adjacent sunroom, so they can easily be rearranged to open up the rooms for larger gatherings. Larger chairs—designed by Tineke—are set against the wall, dressed in a geometric pattern from ZAK+FOX.

Above: In the living room, a contemporary console from Hellman Chang is placed prominently in full view. "If it's the first thing you see, it better be sexy," says Tineke.

The dining room perfectly illustrates the ethos of the project, its warm interior and traditional furnishings offset by a bold light fixture, black crown moldings, and a show-stopping carpet. Yet closer inspection yields the method that makes it all work—a careful layering of texture and pattern in which each piece relates to the next. A monochromatic palette provides a counterweight to the Schumacher wallpaper's large, bold pattern. The smaller patterns on the window coverings pick up the wall color, offset its bold shapes with a smaller, more delicate design, and provide a visual bridge to the textured white light fixture and sideboard.

Then there's the carpet, which Tineke custom designed based on a photograph of moving water that incorporated just the right tones and sense of movement. "It's as if the blues and rusts of the living and dining rooms have dripped off the walls and puddled together onto the floor," says Tineke. "It is exactly the type of juxtaposition of contemporary and traditional design the team was looking for."

The color palette deftly shifts throughout the house, reflecting the energy level of each room. Sophisticated shades of blue, rust, and persimmon in the living and dining rooms shift to more playful tones of marine blue and orange in the kitchen and family room. Upstairs, each bedroom wears its own individual interpretation of the palette: soft, soothing blues and grays in the master bedroom, deep reds and navy in the son's room, and in the daughter's room, a palette of sophisticated pastels drawn from artful paisley window coverings.

Throughout the home, Triggs artfully combines edgy statement lighting—a gorgeous Zia Priven chandelier in the living room, Ron Dier selenite crystal chandelier in the dining room, a striking geometric fixture in the breakfast nook, and Ralph Lauren for Visual Comfort pendants in the kitchen that artfully blend industrial form with glamorous finishes—with traditional furnishings for a striking effect.

Tineke is passionate about every element of her designs, but she has a particular affinity for art and for lighting, which she calls "jewelry for the home." And she absolutely loves jewelry.

Opposite: True to form, a striking black-and-white geometric pendant from Erich Ginder Studio in the breakfast nook lends just the right amount of edge to the dainty Villa Nova print on the window coverings behind it. **Above:** In the kitchen, the living room's soft blues and persimmon become brighter and more playful tones of orange and marine blue. The cabinets are painted a soft dove gray to balance the brighter hues. Pendants from Ralph Lauren for Visual Comfort gracefully merge industrial references with refined finishes.

"MY JOB IS TO CREATE ENVIRONMENTS WHERE MY CLIENTS CAN LIVE OUT THEIR PERSONAL STORIES. I ENCOURAGE THEM TO PUSH THE ENVELOPE JUST ENOUGH SO THAT THEIR HOMES REFLECT WHO THEY ARE AT THEIR MOST CREATIVE. MY BACKGROUND IN SALES HELPS ME CONVINCE THEM TO GO FOR IT."

Above: The husband's office feels like a men's suit, with an expansive U-shaped desk, gray flannel walls, and wallpaper by Philip Jeffreys employed as a wainscot. Tineke calls this room "a man cave in the best possible way." **Opposite:** A tiny office space between the kitchen and ground-floor master bedroom gives the wife a private working space. The open-back desk chair is traditional with a twist, saving both physical and visual space and allowing the beautifully patterned Pierre Frey wallpaper to peek through.

Above: In Tineke's view, bedrooms should be sanctuaries. Softness reigns in this bedroom with a palette of soft blues and grays, and walls are wrapped in softly textured wallpaper from Philip Jeffries.

Opposite top: In the spa-like master bath, an accent wall tiled in a trellis pattern from La Maison provides plenty of visual interest, but the hushed monochromatic hue keeps it from becoming busy.

Right: Deep walnut cabinetry combined with light walls and countertops provides a sense of quiet elegance.

Above: The window coverings in the daughter's room—lively paisley with delicate ball-fringe trim—inspired the color palette of lavender, persimmon, soft gray, pink, and seafoam. The "princess bed" is covered in lavender velvet, the daughter's favorite color. **Opposite:** In the son's bedroom, the themes of blue and red trend stronger and a bit more masculine, paired with leather nightstands and vintage lacrosse sticks. A band of deep red derived from the window coverings' geometric waves forms a bold wainscot.

MAVERICK ROMANCE

For a radical renovation of a mid-century modern house in Silicon Valley, architect TRG Architecture + Design synthesized existing parallels in Californian mid-century design and Australian contemporary design to conceive a home that is fresh, light-filled, and thoroughly connected to its environment.

The creative team, including interior designer Tineke Triggs and landscape architect Michael Callen, transformed the property into an estate-like compound with a beach-house feel. Throughout the project, references to the homeowners' history—they met on the world-famous Bondi Beach—and the husband's native Australia create a thematic through line that speaks to this family and their place in the world.

The architect's program included adding 1,600 square feet on either end of the home to accommodate a wine room, theater, and primary suite, and changing the roofline to include an iconic butterfly shape. A poolhouse—a clean-lined glass pavilion inspired by the lifeguard towers on Bondi Beach—was added to anchor the resort-like pool and outdoor entertaining area. Tineke was tasked with transforming the vibe and personalizing the home's story.

First, primary spaces were lightened, brightened, and opened up. Walls were removed, and dark floors and finishes were replaced with bleached oak flooring and a neutral palette. The result is a modern, laid-back, and accessible aesthetic that creates a serene backdrop for moments of interest. Tineke then focused on imbuing the home with texture and personality, adding pops of color and layering in beach references, some subtle, some overt.

"This house has a lot of layers, mostly in tones of light gray and warmer blues with some jewel tones," she explains. "We picked consistent colors and added playful elements. We also brought in greenery in plants. There are huge palm trees outside, and we wanted to bring that influence inside. The house is all about that connection to the outdoors."

Thinking contemporary beach house, Tineke chose outdoor fabrics for durability and added textural elements like bespoke coffee tables

and chairs in organic shapes with interesting wrappings. Where a Gray Malin photograph of Bondi Beach hangs over the living-room fireplace, a custom rug in ocean blue and white "feels like water flowing through." In the dining area, the Cloud chandelier evokes an inverted jellyfish; the TV room pendant resembles a sea urchin, or coral head. The mudroom entry has a beach-cottage feel, its white shiplap wall hung with straw hats. From the blue tones of the kitchen's reflective glass wall to the powder room's opalescent pearl-like tiles and shell-shaped sconces, references to a watery world wash up throughout the house. In the contemporary poolhouse, one guest room is wallpapered in an exuberant tropical palm pattern; another has paddles mounted on a leaf-print wallpaper. The powder room wallpaper, arrayed with swimmers, adds color and whimsy.

The primary bedroom features a built-in bed, chest of drawers, and side tables with echoes of a ship's stateroom. "There," says Tineke, "the wood is a beach-gray tone, like driftwood from the beach after it has been in the water and grayed out in the sun." Just outside, where glass doors under the sloped butterfly room slide open to create a one-with-nature space, an indoor-outdoor shower speaks to beach life. Other colors in the palette are inspired by marine life and include pops of yellow "for a citrus look."

One of the most magical statements in the project is a bathroom off the gym, two walls of which contain a mural that transports the viewer to a tropical beach replete with colorful beach umbrellas and surf-warning flags. For this feature, partially glassed in for the shower, Tineke had an art photograph printed on waterproof vinyl. Its shades of blue, from aqua to marine, carry the eye to the horizon and beyond— the perfect antidote to a beach-less beach house.

Tineke's approach, one of the statement moments within a serene palette, "is successful in balancing the dance between masculine and feminine." She says, "I like to get attention, but I don't like to be the center of attention, and that speaks to my design. I like comfortable and beautiful, but not so over-the-top that it's frenetic. If a room is over-designed, it makes it hard to relax.

"It's so important that your home be a place to get away from the craziness of the world. You can have statement rooms like a powder room, but you need the rest to be calm and to be about the people who live there."

"THE GOAL WAS TO BRING A LITTLE BIT OF AUSTRALIA TO THE BAY AREA. I FIND THIS HOUSE EXTREMELY DREAMY— IT'S ALL ABOUT CONNECTING TO THE OUTDOORS."

Australia meets America in this midcentury modern manse in Silicon Valley. Tineke worked with her clients to make their home personal and filled with references to their lives together, creating comfortable, vibrant, and meaningful living spaces that are light, bright, and layered. The Ironies Cloud chandelier and white leather Garrett dining chairs from Crosshatch skew contemporary in the almost all-white dining room. The dining table and credenza are from ERINN V.

Above: In the family entry, an array of hats continues the evocation of the Austalia-meets-California lifestyle.

Left: A casual room for hanging out and watching TV is treated in white shiplap paneling and accessorized with the sea-urchin pendant from Coup d'État. The coffee table and bench are from Future Perfect. The wicker egg chair adds a laid-back midcentury feel.

Opposite: The blue glass backsplash "looks like a pool of tropical water," says the designer. "The reflective glass wall is beautiful, and we matched the chairs to go with it." The bar stools are from Cliff Young, the dining chairs from Craft Associates Furniture. The big skylight lets light onto the island, while the kitchen opens directly to the outside dining.

Opposite: The owner's bedroom opens onto the garden and is awash in light. The textural wall covering from Phillip Jeffries and integrated headboard, end tables, and dresser create a soothing backdrop for a restful sleep. The pendants are from Gubi, and the rug is from Perennials. **Above:** The owner's bathroom is light, bright, and serene and, as with almost every other room in the house, opens directly to the outdoors. Cirrus sconces from Coil + Drift, hardware from Hoffman.

Opposite: For a glassed-in shower in the main house with direct access to the pool area, Tineke installed colorful custom waterproof wallpaper from AquaBumps. **Top left:** A water theme flows through the house, appearing intermittently in tones of blue and white. A guest room doubles as the owner's office and features a custom chaise and table from Flexform. "It's a quiet space where he can sit and work when not at his desk," says the designer. "It's a nice quiet moment." **Top right:** In this home, one never feels far from the beach. The laundry room wall is hand-painted with waves by artist Caroline Lizarraga. **Above:** The family room, situated off the kitchen, combines a custom sofa with a coffee table from Future Perfect.

The living is easy in the indoor/outdoor pool house, a contemporary glass pavilion inspired by the lifeguard towers on Bondi Beach. To the side of the pool, furniture from Restoration Hardware, CB2, and Harbour Outdoor creates plenty of seating opportunities. An outdoor kitchen and covered living area also offer various configurations for gatherings large and small. "The owners love to entertain," says Tineke. "The idea was to be able to bring a lot of friends over."

Top left: Beach and ocean references continue in the navy-blue-and-white palette and vintage oars mounted on the wall.

Left: The whimsical swimmer wallpaper from WallsNeedLove references the husband's Australian roots and the beach where they first met. The bubble sconce and WorkOf mirror keep the vibe simple— just the way life should be at the beach.

Opposite: Large-scale palm-leaf wallpaper from Hinson Icons Collections conveys all the richness and color of a tropical landscape in the pool house guest room.

BAYFRONT
DEBONAIRE

When Tineke Triggs approaches a project, the starting point is always the clients: their passions, hobbies, lifestyle, and art. In a home for a client with a sophisticated aesthetic, the challenge was to create a bachelor pad that didn't feel like one from a high-quality, well-built home that was sadly lacking in character.

The homeowner had purchased a 5,000-square-foot house overlooking San Francisco Bay when he asked Tineke to apply her client-forward design skills to the home's primary spaces. "Because he's a single guy who's really into cars and racing," Tineke explains, "I thought about choosing furniture as I'd think about him buying vintage and modern cars. A Vladimir Kagan chair is like a Ferrari—it's an iconic piece that has an aerodynamic feel. The two rounded 1965 Italian chairs are another classic, more like a 1965 Ford Mustang."

Commanding a prime spot facing the view next to the rectilinear fireplace, the high-back Kagan chair's sweeping lines are upholstered in smooth ocean-blue leather and held aloft by expressive wooden legs. It's a touchstone piece in a home that plays on the high style of iconic car designs, the colors of the bay outside the window, and an exceptional collection of contemporary art.

While the structure's siting, upside-down program, and interior spaces were already established, its lack of charisma presented as a clean slate. Other than turning an alcove off the dining room into a sitting room through the addition of built-in bookcases, no big moves were called for. That allowed Tineke to focus on creating spaces with flair.

A wingback chair by Vladimir Kagan sets the tone for a house designed for a car and racing enthusiast. "It feels like a race car chair," says the designer, and its color speaks to the sky and the Bay. The vintage rounded chairs, low-backed so as not to impede the view, are by Dino Frigerio. Tineke transformed an awkwardly empty corner into a cozy lounging spot and balanced the asymmetry of the fireplace and window with an array of graphic black-and-white artworks. The tall hutch helps anchor the space. The custom rug designed by Tineke is visible through the glass-topped coffee table.

The entry sequence was unusual; guests are immediately ushered upstairs to access the views. It was also constrained; any interventions had to be impactful without taking up space. Tineke relied on artwork placed under the open stairway to draw visitors upstairs, then invested the foyer with dramatic details. A dark console table with sculptural brass footings sets off an abstracted landscape painting whose blue-green water and pastel-streaked sky presage the views that await.

Tineke designed a flanking pair of sconces as artfully composed clusters of bronze octahedrons between which amber light glows. The shapes are intriguing, simultaneously evoking the structure of a honeycomb, the textured walls of a cave, rough lava, and fine jewelry.

Upstairs, rooms are awash in the influence of sky and water. Tineke references those influences throughout: in the "rainfall" of glass pendants in the stairwell; in the ice cube–like shapes of the dining-room chandelier; in the library's whale-skeleton wallpaper; and in the blue-and-white palette. Swirling waters, tide lines, the impression water makes on a beach where the outline of the last wave lingers before vanishing into the sand—these are evoked through pillows, textiles, and a white side table with striations of blue created by hand-dipped

Opposite: The white, cream, and blue rug and Drip/Fold side table from Noble Goods continue the ocean theme. The table's markings, made with hand-dripped liquid resin in shades of blue, evoke waves or tide lines. Notes the designer: "I will play with scale in components. So if I have something with a large geometric pattern, the rug will take the opposite approach and vice versa. I like to blend scale in places to make places feel a little less complex and busy." **Above top:** The intriguingly Cubist Welles Chandelier from Gabriel Scott adds sculptural drama to the dining room, as do three-dimensional cabinet doors on a buffet from Hewn's ERINN V. Collection. Tineke paired chairs from Dmitriy & Co with Hellman Chang's Meridian table. Interesting objets and colorful art from the homeowners' collection imbue the room with personality. **Above bottom:** The water references are carried throughout the house, seen here in the raindrop-like pendants in the stairwell.

liquid resin. A custom rug in gray, cream, and blue with bold geometry carries its own movement.

A master of proportion and balance, Tineke loves a challenge. She found one in the asymmetrical arrangement of the fireplace and the living room's competing orientations. She balanced the fireplace wall by creating hearthside seating under the window and extending a line of graphic artwork above the mantle to the opposite side. She offset the high window with a tall cabinet; its dark tone and height help ground the room against the open expanse. Finally, she designed a custom sectional open to both fireplace and views, neatly creating a space that's inviting, comfortable, and functional.

The home is furnished with well-thought-out details in perfect proportions, from the dining room buffet with its three-dimensional front to the airy breakfast nook with its tulip table, bubble chandelier, and vibrant art. A primary bedroom with a quiet hillside view features lighting that evokes wind chimes; a retreat-like bath exudes serenity. Impeccably arranged art and objects reference the owner's history and travels.

This is a project in which the designer never lost sight of her client. Just as she found the perfect spot for butterflies he'd collected, Tineke celebrated his interests and passions. "He's an engineer," she says. "Some of these objects—like the dining room light fixture, the gear-like legs on a table, and the aerodynamic structure of the dining room console—play to that."

Her love of unique detail sets the project apart. "I almost always create something custom," she

says. "I think it's because I never find one hundred percent what I need. Often the original isn't customizable, isn't the right size, isn't the right finish, or isn't quite what I had envisioned. I think the artist in me wants to create something inspired by elements of other things. And I just like to have things be a little bit unique. For me, it's always been about creating and being an artist."

In this house on the hillside, that artistry shines.

Above: A clean and vibrant space, the breakfast nook is the perfect place to wake to the day. The off-white Eero Saarinen table, light gray Arrmet Studio chairs, and vintage bubble chandelier set a calm tone while the bold orange, yellow, and blue of the art bring the zing.

Opposite: The designer turned an underutilized space off the dining room into a compact library/TV room by creating two bookshelves (one of which hides a television behind sliding doors) flanking the large window. The whale-skeleton wallpaper ("Bruce" from Abnormals Anonymous) adds a glam edginess to the space.

"THE HOME IS A REFLECTION OF PLACE, WITH VIEWS FROM SAUSALITO OUT TO THE OCEAN. THERE'S A LOT OF FOG IN SAUSALITO, SO YOU'RE THINKING ABOUT BRINGING FOG AND WATER INTO YOUR PALETTE TO BLEND INTO THE ENVIRONMENT THERE. WHEN I HAVE A HOUSE WITH A LOT OF VIEWS, I TRY HARD TO MAKE THE FURNITURE INTERESTING BUT ALSO BLEND IN."

Opposite: Teneke's extra-tall custom headboard creates balance in a room with ten-foot-tall ceilings. An array of pendant lights from Vibia add interest while further balancing the verticality of the space. Blue and white textiles carry the Bay's tidal vibe into the home's private areas.

Above and right: The primary bathroom already had an existing vessel tub placed near the large window. Tineke added a Phillip Jeffries wallcovering and open wood shelving matching the floating vanity to provide storage without sacrificing the room's light and airy sanctuary feel.

GLAM GETAWAYS

MOUNTAIN
MODERN

Tahoe mountain style has long been characterized by gabled roofs, heavy wood logs and timbers, stone fireplaces, and earthy colors. As technologies have improved and tastes shifted, however, homeowners and their creatives have pushed the definition of the genre toward one of flat roofs, clean lines, oversized windows, and contemporary furnishings.

Martis Camp, a luxury enclave located on the north shore of Lake Tahoe with private access to the lake, downhill skiing, and its own golf course, was one of the first Tahoe developments that had a big range, from the classic A-frame cabin to extremely contemporary designs. "These clients leaned much more minimalist," says Tineke, "so we brought in feelings of warmth through lots of wood-paneled walls and some interesting details."

The four-bedroom, two-story structure of wood, glass, and blackened steel was designed by architect Clare Walton on a gently sloping tree-backed site within view of Martis Camp's party barn. The clients, a Bay Area family of five, had already been working with Julie Zener of Zener Schon Contemporary Art to select works that were, in Tineke's words, "avant-garde and unexpected and edgy, which I love."

It is the art that kicks off the interior experience. It makes an impression from the moment of entry in large abstract paintings. This continues with statement pieces such as the painting in the dining room, a sort of contemporary riff on wildlife art, two works in the hallway reminiscent of topographic maps or abstract landscape photographs, and a black-and-white painting of bold swoops, arcs, and curves that injects energy into the otherwise serene primary bedroom.

Tineke's creative contributions play off the art, add warmth and texture (essential in a glassy modern mountain home), and reveal a few surprises. Where the staircase meets the dining area, for instance, Tineke designed a custom punched metal railing "to add a little bit more interest to the dining room" and to create a sense of separation from the transitional spaces of entry and stairwell. An upstairs loft space became the game/family room where she installed exuberant turquoise game chairs that perfectly match the hues in the painting that hangs in the space. Below the game room, in an alcove off a hallway that had no apparent use, Tineke created a compact office behind a sliding door. "It was this small no man's land," she says. "Little did we know prior to the pandemic that the space would be used so much."

The palette is neutral throughout, grounded in the living room with a massive and inviting brown sectional, kitchen cabinetry that leans light gray, and region-appropriate materials like wool, leather, and hide. Wood ceilings and floors warm the space without making it dark or heavy.

For a Marin family's new home at Martis Camp, a four-season getaway on the north end of Lake Tahoe, Tineke was tasked with creating a comfortable contemporary interior with a dash of the playful to complement architect Clare Walton's modern rustic design. The board-formed concrete fireplace and custom brown-wool-upholstered sectional work well with the modern architecture. The metal frames of the accent chairs look like branches, while the stone interlocking-gear pieces, sourced from Stone Yard, as coffee table are a great conversation piece.

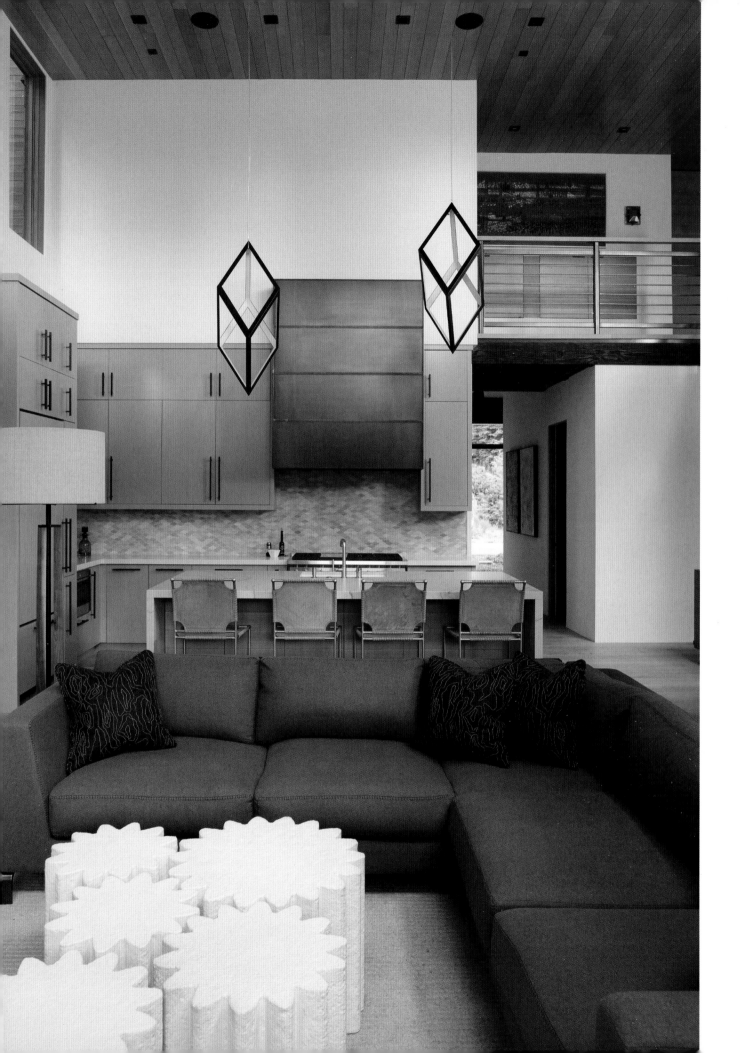

As for furnishings, forget wildlife sculptures and antler chandeliers. The mountain, game, and North Woods references are oh-so-subtle. They're found in fur throw pillows and an accent pillow stitched in a bark pattern, Pendleton wool fabrics and leather locker handles in the bunk room, and a decidedly glam console at the base of the stairs whose metal inlay looks like growth rings from the cross-section of a tree.

In a whimsical nod to skiing, the wood backs of the dining chair are reminiscent of crossed ski tips. Otherwise, the decor is unapologetically modern: board-formed concrete fireplaces, angular lighting, a blackened steel range hood, and light-bathed marble and glass bathrooms within a bleached-oak palette. The centerpiece of the living room is a sculptural installation of five stone "gears," arranged so they're interlocking, in lieu of a coffee table.

Opposite: Christopher Boots ORP pendants deliver the unexpected; they can change color and can be set to music. "You can see them from the barn of Martis Camp, and you can have a lot of fun with them," says Tineke. "They made them red, white, and blue on the Fourth of July." The cowhide counter chairs with whip-stitching add a western vibe without being obvious.

Above right: A narrow alcove was cleverly adapted as an office, with wall paneling and a sliding door to elevate and differentiate the space. The workspace with its tall desk chair is centered under one high window—perfect for the new work-from-home movement.

Right: In the dining area, a Cliff Young dining table and Eco Leather X Chairs, which have a crisscrossing wood frame reminiscent of crossed ski tips. The Phasmida light fixture is from Christopher Boots.

As in every Tineke Triggs interior, lighting is show-stopping and selected to add interest without interfering with the forest-and-mountain views. Glamorous jewelry-like clusters in dark brass emit an amber glow in the hallway. Minimal rhombus-shaped pendants (programmable to light up in color) hang at an angle over the kitchen island. A multi-branched pendant inspired by walking stick insects and suspended from the wood ceiling of the dining area speaks to nature most abstractly.

This is a new take on mountain modern that speaks to place while performing a delicate balancing act between light and dark, openness and enclosure, indoor and outdoor. Says Tineke, "It's a contemporary twist on the Tahoe vibe."

Above: Connection to the outdoors is important at this luxury enclave located on the north shore of Lake Tahoe. Throughout the home, art is a big part of the program. Tineke and the owners worked with Tara Schon and Julie Zener of Zener Schon Contemporary Art.

Opposite: Tineke created an energy-infused space by upholstering chairs from Four Hands in a bright blue Pindler fabric to pick up the colors in the vibrant Ashleigh Sumner painting. The game table is from Taracea.

Right: Bleached walnut and marble combine in the calming primary bath. "I love the warmth of the wood and the floating vanity. There's open space for towels, yet you still have storage below. It gives it a less heavy feeling. The space is long and narrow, and the architect devised a clever way to deal with it: The shower has a half wall, then the half wall becomes the faucet for the tub. The tub and the shower both get the view out the window, so they're not competing."

Below: Tineke solved the twin-or-king-bed conundrum by creating movable twin beds unified by a single headboard. "That second guest bedroom is often challenging for people; they're not sure if they want it to be a king bed or twins to overflow with the bunk room. We've done this a few times, where you take two beds and create one headboard then the twins roll to become a king. It makes the room more versatile."

Opposite: The home's modern mountain architecture strategically uses wood on the headboard wall in the primary bedroom. Fur pillows glam it up. The Hillary Platform Bed is from Vanguard and nightstands are from Mr. Brown. The Bilbao Fishtail Pendant is from Arteriors Home.

"THE CHALLENGE WAS TO BRING IN ELEMENTS OF SURPRISE, COZINESS, AND COMFORT IN A MODERN LINEAR HOME. THE CLIENTS LOVE BEING UP THERE BUT DIDN'T WANT A TRADITIONAL TAHOE VIBE. WE WANTED THE INTERIORS TO FIT WITH TAHOE AND THE MOUNTAINS—BUT BE MORE CONTEMPORARY."

CAMP GETAWAY

Every house has a vibe, and this house's vibe is decidedly playful. As is often the case, Tineke designed this house in the mountains of Lake Tahoe for clients she had worked with before and knew well. It was the husband's long-held dream to have a vacation home for their family of five. After searching for several years, they zeroed in on Martis Camp outside the town of Truckee as the perfect location for their family.

This house would be home to young children and often filled with friends, so Tineke took a path less traveled. Knowing her clients loved color, textures, and patterns, she embraced an alternative take on the expected mountain modern design. Tineke embraces color, playing with the scale of textures and patterns throughout the open-plan house in much the same way that a composer arranges the notes of a musical composition.

"When you're looking at any room, you will see the connections. It's almost as if you can take a string and connect the dots throughout the house," says Tineke. "This is how I ensure each piece lives harmoniously with the others, each engaging the other in a visual conversation."

A perfect example of this visual conversation is the open space that connects the living room, dining room, and kitchen. There are three light fixtures in the vertical space, each playing a complementary role in the overall conversation. In the living room, a leggy, modern pendant gives a slight nod to the rings of antlers found in many traditional mountain homes, three sleek, contemporary rings hang above the dining table, and the shimmering geometric shapes of a Gabriel Scott pendant float above the island in the kitchen. A consistent palette of dark metals keeps them all in the same key.

The color palette in the main living spaces—a blend of chocolate and red, with hints of green—takes its cue from the mountain surroundings. While the browns and greens are drawn from the landscape, the red is inspired by Martis Camp's red barn—an iconic presence in this resort community. The color also pops against the green of the surrounding forest, and as Tineke points out, red is a symbol of good luck in Asian cultures.

This is, above all, a vacation home. Frequently filled with visitors, it needs to be comfortable and functional and an easy place for guests to feel at home. Custom-designed glass wine storage fills a niche beneath the stairs, guest bedrooms are warm and inviting, and open shelving stacked with everyday dishes allows guests to easily find what they need to serve themselves. Of course, Tineke asserts, "every Tahoe house has to have a bunk room." In this house, the bunks are red, configured with two queen beds and two twins for maximum flexibility. Curtains in a lively wave pattern pull together all of the colors in the house.

Above: On the island and pantry, wood planks in a chevron pattern hint at a barn vernacular without being too rustic. A Gabriel Scott fixture in dark bronze and gunmetal provides a chic contrast to the more traditional white cabinetry.

Opposite top: In the open space that connects the living room, dining room and kitchen, each of the light fixtures plays a complementary role in the overall conversation.

Opposite bottom left: A wine cellar was high on her clients' wish list, so Tineke tucked glass-encased wine storage into the L-shaped space underneath the stairs.

Opposite bottom right: In the powder room, a dramatic dragon wallpaper is offset with pendants from Jonathan Browning and a metal wainscot.

Perhaps no space expresses this home's overall vibe better than the game room. Designed for a family with young children, it is decidedly jubilant. The room's epicenter is the large, navy sectional sofa that easily accommodates family movie nights and the making of forts. Ottomans are an invitation to go ahead and bounce, and board game artwork pulls it all together. A palette of navy, orange, and purple is simply hands-down fun.

"This room is all about that," insists Tineke.

One short year after completing the main house, the family found themselves hosting so often that they decided they needed a guesthouse. Besides providing room for more visitors, the idea was to create a party pad where the adults could hang out after the kids go to bed. The guesthouse is not large, but it is definitely lively—a joy-filled space for kids and parents alike.

The smaller space provided the opportunity for a departure from the design of the main house. Light, fun colors underscore the party atmosphere, with yellows, blues, and pinks drawn from the large, abstract plaid that covers the sofa cushions—one of Tineke's patterns. The glass tile above the bar and the adjacent reflective wallpaper reinforce the party atmosphere with the slightest note of a disco ball.

In the main gathering room, a rolling cart that serves as an island for the open kitchen is easily rolled out of the way to accommodate a crowd, and a light-filled eating area embraces the views of the woods. In a testament to Tineke's seemingly never-ending ingenuity, she custom-designed the sofa that floats in the center of the space to face in three directions at once, so no one ever has to miss a thing. To make room for the equally ingenious hidden dartboard, the sofa seat slides forward to provide players with a clear shot. Priorities, as always, are in order.

Top and bottom left: The guest rooms—in complementary color schemes—employ an ingenious use of space, with floating side tables and, in one room, twin mattresses mounted on sliding casters, so they can be slid apart or together to form a king bed under the shared headboard. **Opposite:** "Every Tahoe house should have a red bunk room!" says Tineke. In place of the usual ladder, custom steps access the upper bunks, with storage tucked below.

Above: The guesthouse game room wears its identity on its sleeve. Behind the copious sofa, a game table from Vanguard is wrapped with a colorful mosaic of fabrics, topped with glass for protection, and surrounded by chairs echoing the colors of the game board artwork. An appropriately quirky pendant—fabricated from an old street sign—hangs above.

Right: The game room's riot of colors is perfectly balanced, anchored by the custom sectional from Robert Allen in navy. Cabinets in what Tineke calls "the perfect shade of gray" form a cool and collected backdrop.

Above: A multifunctional party room fit for both adults and children, the guest house's great room gives equal weight to form and function. Tones of blue, pink, and yellow keep it fun. Flexible furniture, like the custom-designed sofa that anchors the space, accommodate a party.

Opposite: The dining alcove is a magical space filled with light reflected in smoked glass pendants from Allied Maker.

"OUR IDEA FROM THE BEGINNING WAS TO TURN THE HOUSE INTO A MODERN TAKE ON THE LAKE TAHOE VACATION HOUSE VIBE. THIS IS A PLACE TO PLAY."

Opposite: A palette of lime green and playful patterned wallpaper enlivens a guesthouse bedroom.

Above: In a guest bathroom, a custom-designed pattern of contrasting blue and white tiles seems to break away and travel up the wall.

A PLACE
TO PLAY

This beachfront house—set on a remarkable site at the end of the Seadrift Lagoon at Stinson Beach with endless views of both the water and the mountains—is a Cinderella story. A short drive from the family's city house but seemingly a world away, this is an airy, welcoming retreat perfect for family, friends, and relaxed entertaining. But it wasn't always that way.

The clients—a couple with four children who had worked with Tineke on their home in San Francisco—were looking for something entirely different for their beachfront getaway. She grew up in Malibu, he is a surfer, and they both wanted to give their children the freedom and joy of growing up near the ocean. They had been renting in Stinson Beach for fifteen years and looked at dozens of properties before they found their house.

The home they set their heart on dated from the 1970s—think dark wood paneling, small windows, tiled countertops, and maple cabinetry everywhere. On top of it all, the original house barely acknowledged the adjacent lagoon. "It was like a time capsule, preserved in all its original glory," says Tineke. "But the potential and the views—they were amazing!"

Tineke collaborated with architect Stacey Ford and builder George Flynn—both located in the small beach town and well-versed in the coastal environment. The team loved the flow of the U-shaped house, which encircles a protected entry courtyard (a blessing in an often windy beachfront location), but everything else had to go. So they embarked on a complete transformation, creating a home that embraces the views and the active lifestyle of this modern family of six, but still exudes a subtle 1970s vibe that speaks to the home's roots.

On the coast of Northern California, the colors of the landscape are often muted, tempered by the ever-present mist and fog. Accordingly, the exterior is finished in a soft gray stain, nearly disappearing into the view. Inside, Tineke embraced the coastal environment with a palette of soft grays and blues that coexist perfectly with bright white walls and ceilings of bleached oak. Soft gray concrete floors are durable, easily handling the sand tracked in regularly. Black doors and windows, dark hardware, and kitchen cabinets coated in an ebony stain add depth and balance (not unlike punctuation marks in a well-crafted sentence).

Throughout the house, a sense of relaxed serenity reigns, perhaps nowhere more than in the primary bedroom. Inspired by the coastal landscape, its palette softened by mist and fog, the bedroom is entirely given over to the view outside the expansive windows.

Whether indirectly through color and texture or directly by capturing the various views, every space in the house engages the landscape. In what would prove to be a transformative decision, the design team blew out the three small windows in the living room that provided meager glimpses of the adjacent lagoon, replacing them with a massive pair of picture windows that open an entire corner of the room to the view. That singular decision creates a focal point that grounds the house in its spectacular site, functioning as an ever-changing work of art.

Designed for use, the flow through the home is easy, and though restful, it can easily

accommodate family and friends. Everything has a place, and every bit of space is put to use. The living room is a serene place to gather and take in the full glory of the view. The kitchen, opened up to create more space, boasts a generous island and skylights that allow light to stream into the interior.

The sunroom off the kitchen is now a breakfast room with a killer vista. The guest room cleverly includes a home office that forms a sweet vignette. Hidden behind a sliding barn door, a mudroom with access to the outdoors is set midway between the children's rooms, providing the perfect drop spot for sandy, wet clothes. And off the detached garage, a rumpus room combines hangout space with more sleeping accommodations,

enabling this modest house to host a crowd.

"It's so important to connect to the family, to the architecture, and to the site," says Tineke. "I've now had the opportunity to work with this family in two very different places and create environments that reflect and support how they live their lives both in the city and at the beach."

Above: An iconic mid-century chair is a statement piece, but it defers to the view by not taking up too much space, either physically or visually. The geometric pattern of the white Ann Sacks tile surrounding the central fireplace geometric is a subtle nod to the home's original decade.

Opposite: The vibe is coastal, casual, and comfortable throughout. The artwork is Elm Cetacean, a woodblock print by Julian Meredith.

Above: Floating shelves and peekaboo windows just above the counters let in the northern light. "Floating shelves are perfect in a weekend house," says Tineke. "Guests can see just what they need and help themselves."

Top right: The new breakfast nook, once a sunroom, boasts a breathtaking view.

Bottom right: In the kitchen, light and dark tones exist in balance: Lower cabinets wear an ebony stain, and the black stove is a standout.

Opposite: Tineke gave new life to what was once a dark den. It is now a guest suite with a large sliding door to the courtyard that also incorporates a small home office, creating a charming vignette.

Above left: Planked interior doors, like this one leading to the mudroom/laundry room, reinforce the message that this is a casual house.

Above right: A custom Fireclay tile pattern, in colors that reflect both land and sea, tumbles down the wall in the guest bath.

Right: In the girls' room, two full beds outfitted with trundles accommodate sleepovers. Hints of pink and delicate tassels on the blankets and on the Anthropologie pendants are feminine without being frilly.

*"WE DESIGNED
THIS HOME TO BE
FILLED WITH KIDS
AND FRIENDS.
IT'S A PLACE
TO UNWIND. A
PLACE TO PLAY."*

Top left: Tineke worked with local metal fabricator Steel Geisha to create the ceiling-mounted towel bar in front of this bathroom's frosted window.

Bottom left: Everything is clean, contemporary, and easily accessible, with loads of open shelving.

Opposite: Off the detached garage, a new rumpus room holds the television as well as huge sofas that can shed their back cushions and convert to twin beds, enabling this modest house to host a crowd.

SURF
SCENE

This project—a beachfront bungalow with views of the western slopes of Mount Tamalpais in the laid-back town of Stinson Beach—is the perfect getaway for its owners, a family of five. Fortuitously purchased just before the pandemic, the home is a sanctuary for this surfing family whose happy place is on the coast. Tineke knows the family well. In fact, she designed their house in San Francisco, which sits right next door to her own.

"They are my next-door neighbors," jokes Tineke. "I had to get this right!"

Tucked behind the dunes, the small three-bedroom house—which the family purchased prior to buying their larger home in the city—is a 1960s bungalow with a distinctively vintage vibe. Tineke and her clients immediately agreed that they wanted to keep that quirky feel of the interior, which captured just what the family was looking for in their coastal getaway.

To accomplish this, they elected to update the exterior, its now more contemporary lines covered in site-appropriate horizontal cedar siding that will age in place. Working with Brian Koch of Terra Ferma Landscapes, they transformed the central courtyard that acts as both the home's primary entry and its central outdoor gathering place in this often windy beachfront setting. Now seamlessly integrated into the indoor-outdoor flow of the house, the courtyard effectively expands the living spaces without changing the footprint of the L-shaped house.

Though the period feel remains, the flow of the house is vastly improved. To fit an eating area into the existing triangular space that directly overlooks the beach, Tineke expanded the house into the existing courtyard just enough to shift the kitchen and create room for a dining

table and chairs. To help keep the interior's 1960s flair intact, Tineke embraced the funky angles of the great room's original trusses, simply painting them white and leaving them alone.

Inside and out, this house is all about the beach and the view, which dictate the flow, neutral color scheme, and material choices. The home's palette is filled with texture-driven neutrals, vintage finds, and quirky details, with durability always front of mind. Beadboard walls and gray-washed oak form a visually consistent backdrop. Indoor/outdoor rugs throughout the house provide the traditional sisal look with the durability of polyester. Caesarstone countertops in "Pebble" in the kitchen and bathrooms echo the color of the sand and are, according to Tineke, "indestructible."

Since family and friends are constantly running in and out from the beach, nothing could be too precious. Poured concrete floors, vintage furniture in comfortably worn leather, and soft fabrics define the rooms. In fact, given the choice of "a little worn" and "more than a little worn" on the leather living room chairs, the clients opted for "more than a little worn." However, they always chose originals, and classic design meets beach house vintage throughout the house. In the great room,

Embracing the quirky 1960s beach vibe of the original house, Tineke left the great room's original beams intact, simply painting them white.

two classic Danish designs—a set of Spanish Chairs by Børge Mogensen and a Copenhagen Chair by Mogens Voltelen—face each other across the seating area.

"I love how they talk to each other," says Tineke.

Tineke filled the home with fun, authentic vintage pieces that feel as if they could have been handed down across generations, working with Venice Beach-based stylist Cyia Batten—the wife's cousin and lifelong friend.

"We had so much fun shopping for the vintage finds," says Tineke. "Cyia knows the family so well, and she brought a keen eye to the project."

In the small bungalow, space was at a premium, so Tineke tucked custom built-ins into rooms in lieu of furniture to save space. Built-in dresser drawers in bedrooms, floor-to-ceiling custom cabinetry in the master bath, storage under bunks, and bins in the bunkhouse's shared bathroom are a clever use of space.

In this house, where family and friends are always welcome, a detached bunkhouse forms a separate getaway for teenagers and their friends. The multiuse space accommodates a crowd, with a single bunk room in lieu of separate bedrooms, a shared sink area inspired by layouts made popular in many hotels and restaurants, and a lounge designed explicitly for, well, lounging.

"THIS HOUSE IS ALL ABOUT FAMILY, FRIENDS, AND FUN."

Opposite: "I think we have a strong shared understanding of the California lifestyle," says landscape architect Brian Koch of Terra Ferma Landscapes. "The flow of this house and courtyard embraces that easy, family-oriented, indoor/outdoor way of life."

Above: The design process for this unique project was a bit like a treasure hunt. Tineke sourced the concrete pendants above the kitchen island from a small business on Etsy.

Right: The new bar area marks a subtle transition from the kitchen to the dining area.

Top left: A collection of hats on a vintage wood hat rack evokes a life lived outdoors. **Top right:** In the primary bath, a frosted window allows light to flood the room without sacrificing privacy. **Above:** The small primary bedroom, which overlooks the beach, has built-ins with leather pulls that look perfectly at home while conserving space. **Opposite:** Set back-to-back, the two guest bedrooms are all about vintage and textures.

Above: In the bunkroom shower, the playful laser-cut tile reads "surf's up."

Right: In this house designed for family and friends, the separate bunkhouse is a multiuse space designed to accommodate a crowd comfortably.

Opposite: A hidden dartboard and a leather game table that rotates to accommodate six different games provide a lot of fun in very little space.

Left: A trough sink accommodates a crowd and is paired with separate spaces for lavatory and shower. Tineke worked with craftsman Jim Misner to convert piping and pendants into a striking custom light fixture.

Below: The multiuse bunkhouse was designed to sleep as many as possible, with custom built-in beds and bunks draped with Belgian blankets from Uniq'uity.

PARTY
WAVE

With Tineke, so much is about the clients and their story.

"And this is a nice one," she says. "In this family, the husband is a landscape designer and installer, and the whole family loves to surf. Their parents have a place in a little surf community just outside of Aptos, so they knew it well and loved it, but all the homes were built in the 1970s and had little character to them. We wanted to make this feel like a real beach house. It's very different from the clients' traditional house in Palo Alto, and that was intentional. Here we were trying to play into California's beach culture and create a fun environment."

The three-bedroom home is arranged over two levels with the primary living spaces—open plan living room, kitchen and deck—and the primary bedroom on the upper level to best take advantage of the ocean views. The lower level houses the service areas (garage, laundry, storage, outdoor shower), two bedrooms, and the formal entry, which leads guests directly to the stairs and aloft to the view. Since the space is compact, Tineke employed thoughtful strategies to enhance the way the clients would live in the home. Significant interventions included reconfiguring the downstairs space to combine the pantry and laundry room to create a second ensuite bathroom space. She also redesigned the staircase to make a more stylish and exciting sense of arrival.

Tineke is a masterful space planner. After identifying issues with entertaining and flow upstairs, she suggested combining the existing kitchen and a separate small dining room. By eliminating the dining room and extending the kitchen across the back wall to the staircase, she could enlarge the living room while creating one large kitchen, where she sacrificed the kitchen island in favor of a full dining table. The family loves

"IF I'M GOING TO DO NO COLOR, IT HAD BETTER BE TEXTURED. OTHERWISE, THE ROOM WILL FEEL FLAT."

In the living room, a custom art piece resembling an abstraction of rocks at ocean's edge matches the palette of the fabric. "In this case, we wanted a textural element that wouldn't be distracting," explains Tineke. The limestone fireplace surround is from Da Vinci. Verellen sofa with Mark Alexander fabric, Nickey Kehoe spindle-back chairs in bleached oak, custom oak and blackened steel side table from Robert James Collection and custom coffee table from Skylar Morgan.

to cook and frequently entertains; this approach perfectly fits their casual beach lifestyle.

The final intervention was to swap out windows for French doors on the ocean side of the house, enlarge the deck and add a fire pit—essential amenities for indoor/outdoor coastal living.

The clients wanted to forego intense color in this project in favor of a more laid-back beachy vibe, explains Tineke. "Their palettes are all very soothing, timeless, and natural. All the wood colors are in bleached oak to evoke a driftwood palette, effortless in structure but very comfortable. The furniture was all chosen to be comfortable and inviting. I love the serenity of the space."

For inspiration, they looked to Australia, which Tineke describes as "more contemporary than the typical California casual," and several furniture pieces and a light fixture were sourced from the region. Tineke installed a beadboard ceiling in the living room, kitchen, and primary bedroom to add texture and lend a beach-cottage feel. Unexpected details include a hand-crocheted pendant in the kitchen, a rattan pendant in the primary bedroom, dark doors with raffia screens for the closets, and a whimsical blowfish wallpaper in the powder room.

The designer made over a downstairs alcove with 1970s cabinetry as a bar for a gracious hospitality experience. The laundry room/pantry is a playful space meant to inject some fun into household chores, with its whale skeleton wallpaper, beach-umbrella-and-sky artwork, and curtain rod suspended from leather straps. While certain elements repeat throughout the house, at times used in different ways, other variations on a theme create a connection between spaces but with differentiation. One bathroom might have a beaded light, for instance, the next a rope light. In homage to the husband's line of work, Tineke brought in a lot of plants, which soften the space and quite literally bring nature indoors.

This casual-but-refined beach home displays Tineke's deftness with disparate but related elements and her ability to create a dwelling that is light and bright with points of interest and intriguing conversation starters but still suffused with serenity, beauty, and a sense of calm. "You don't have to customize everything to make it look bespoke or unique. You just have to know how to mix and match properly so that they all blend together nicely," she says. "We stayed very consistent in our thread with the linens, the lights and the tones, the white countertops, and dark metal elements."

The result is a much-loved home that gets continuous use from the family and friends. It is unfussy yet full of interesting details and bathed with even light from the east-facing kitchen and the west-facing living room. And despite being frequently filled with an assortment of characters tumbling in wet from the ocean, it is a peaceful refuge. So much so that at the end of the weekend, the wife will often send the family back to the Peninsula so she can work from the beach home for a few more days. It is then that the home reveals how it serves in so many ways. Says Tineke, "It becomes her silent sanctuary."

Above left: Tineke selected the canopy bed in driftwood from Maiden Home and the rattan pendant from My Bali Living. "We kept the palette simple and calming. If we did use colors, they were very soft, nothing bold, with natural fibers for the light fixtures and dark metal finishes. And we used a textured wallpaper."

Above right: In this home, the ocean is never out of mind. The painting above a dresser references the waves hitting the sand, mere steps away.

Left: Plaster walls in the bathroom give a creamy depth without being busy; their water resistance makes them well-suited to ocean areas. In the bathrooms, everything is custom, including the vanities, with a consistency in fixtures and metals from one to the next. "We don't like everything to be exactly the same, but we like them to have a connection to each other." The sconces are from Rose Uniacke Lighting, the custom matte black mirror from Mirror Image Home.

Opposite: A vignette in the kids' bedroom captures the fun and casual spirit of the house.

Opposite: Beachgoers make a pit stop at the cool minimal shower to wash off the sand before coming inside. Matte black shower from PHYLRICH. **Above:** Tineke loves a whimsical wallpaper when the mood calls for it, as seen in the powder room's blowfish wallpaper from Abnormals Anonymous. The mirror is from O & G Studio..

COASTAL CABANA

Tineke Triggs loves Cabo. It was the first foreign place she had ever visited, and she and her husband hope to buy a home there one day. She loves the warmth of the people, the originality of the artisans, the cultural embrace of color and design, the timeless architecture, and the coastal beauty. So when a favorite client—a couple with three daughters—asked her to come to Cabo San Lucas to transform their 5,000-square-foot townhouse into a home with soul, she leaped at the opportunity.

"To do a project in Mexico was a dream for me because I'm in love with everything about the place," she says. "Working on this project, I spent a lot of time in Mexico with the local people, and I got closer to the culture. This family loves the culture just like I do. They've always felt like this is the place where their family could retreat. They come here all the time; it's where they connect on holidays, and when the girls are all grown up, this is where they want to be."

The home sits atop a cliff with dramatic 180-degree views of a seemingly endless ocean. The existing architecture leaned contemporary and somewhat sterile, defined by large volumes treated in stone, stucco, wood and travertine, and glass expanses opening to the outdoors. Accent walls and a ceiling at the entry and interior cabinetry and trim in Mexican walnut added warmth and richness but also lent a dark, heavy feel. The designer's job was to create balance and comfort and infuse the home with the owners' character while still paying homage to place.

On the clients' part, says the wife, the goal was a home that felt "welcoming, comfortable, and relaxing and also incorporated Mexican style into the house without making it feel too traditional or too-of-the-moment trendy." To achieve that, it seemed natural to turn to Tineke. "Aesthetically, I appreciate some of the core elements of her style: her interest in bringing in texture, her layering that keeps things from feeling flat, her marriage of form and function, and her mixing of new and vintage."

Tineke loves Mexico. She leapt at the chance to infuse some soul into a 5,000-square-foot townhome in Cabo. The open-plan living area looks straight out across the patio and past native plantings to the depths of the ocean. References to the region's colors, culture, and handicrafts are found throughout the home. The sectional's rope-wrapped leather frame features two elements that repeat throughout the project, both of which speak to Mexico and the seaside. The surfboard serves as functional art.

These hallmarks of Tineke's style are wildly successful in this Cabo retreat. "There are a couple of directions you can go with creating an environment in a second home that connects you to a culture without being kitschy," Tineke explains. "We tried to vibe into the modern side of Mexican design and the color palette of the coastal feel." Her approach was to keep the palette neutral but dotted with ocean references, then infuse the space with textural elements and moments of contrasting hues in deference to Mexico's love of color and exuberance.

Tineke sourced locally as much as possible to support and draw attention to local vendors, a process that was as fun as it was rewarding. In exploring nearby resources, she discovered a vibrant crafts community in Todos Santos, where she knocked on doors and haunted boutiques to find artisan-made goods such as textiles, as well as manufacturers who could build to her specifications. The nightstands and bed in the primary suite, for instance, were made by Mexican furniture makers, as were the dining table, living room sectional, kitchen stools, and a variety of other pieces.

Tineke focused on adding textural elements to soften the spaces, from lively black-and-white tiles on the kitchen island to natural materials like sisal, leather, wood, textiles, and items that evoke in their shape or materiality seashells, driftwood, and baskets. Surf and beach references are both literal and figurative: shell-edge drapes in the primary bedroom, an artisan surfboard in the living room, an art piece made from coconut shells in the primary bedroom, hanging lights in the shape of shells in the guest room, and large-format ocean photography.

The restraints came off in the girls' bunk room. This lively space has three built-in beds and a sleeper sofa, colorful custom pillows and poufs, a cactus hat rack, and quirky Warhol-like art pieces of Chihuahuas made by a local artist—set against a blue-and-white St. Frank wall covering. On the girls' private patio, two hanging egg chairs and an outdoor ottoman take the relaxed beachy vibe outside.

In addition to masterful space planning and thoughtful attention to function, Tineke's gifts are seen in the details, whether sourced internationally or locally or custom-made from her original designs. She loves to combine things she finds in showrooms or on Etsy with one-of-a-kind items she commissions, whether by high-end craftspeople or local artisans.

She strikes that delicate balance between interest and calm in every interior space. From sanctuary bathrooms to the minimal but stylish outdoor shower to the expansive ocean-facing patio with outdoor dining, lounge with fire pit, and dipping pool set within a desert landscape, the house "is really about how it can serve a lot of people and still have lots of little getaways, with texture and elements connecting it to the ocean and the coastal feel of Mexico."

"SUPPORTING LOCAL ARTISANS IS IMPORTANT FOR SUSTAINABILITY OF CULTURE AND DIVERSITY OF DESIGN. WHEN YOU HAVE A DEVELOPMENT IN A PLACE LIKE THIS, YOU WANT TO SUPPORT LOCAL AGRICULTURE AND LOCAL ARTISANS. YOU'RE RESPONSIBLE FOR BRINGING BACK WEALTH TO THESE COUNTRIES. THAT'S REALLY IMPORTANT TO ME, AND I FEEL THAT WAY EVERYWHERE I DESIGN."

Top right: A trio of baskets on the wall is a nod to the handicrafts Mexico is known for.

Right: Mexican walnut combines with a Caesarstone backsplash and countertops for a warm but fresh look. Stools from RUK Studio are upholstered with fabric from XUN. The graphic black-and-white tiles from clé add texture and a touch of sophisticated whimsy.

The bleached oak table is surrounded by sculptural leather dining chairs, which help soften the strong lines of the architecture. Tineke always seeks out the unexpected in lighting, as in this trio of basket-like pendants.

Above: "That cactus is so insanely incredible," says the designer. "I love it. The outdoor chair looks a little like a clamshell, which is fun." The pillow, made from vintage tapestry, is Mexican.

Right: Beachside references are both literal and figurative: shells stitched onto the edges of drapes, hanging lights that look like clamshells.

Left: The girls' bedroom can accommodate a crowd with three built-in bunks and a sleeper sofa from Ironhorse Home. The clever space-saving design clusters the locally made beds in one corner while using built-in bookshelves to create privacy. Pillows covered in colorful textiles speak to the Mexican love of bold hues. The patterned wall covering is from St. Frank. Vibrant bedspreads feature the embroidery style originated by Otomí artisans in central Mexico.

Above: The home's most playful details include a life-size cactus hung with beach hats, color-infused textiles, and "hola, hola, hola" on the wall.

DESIGNER SHOWCASE

DAVID AND IMAN

A veteran of six San Francisco Decorator Showcase houses, Tineke never disappoints, consistently creating spaces that are inspiring, thought-provoking, and a little edgy. Most importantly, the areas she creates tell a story. When designing a room in a showcase house, she invariably invents a persona—a virtual client, if you will—which enables her to give the room a distinct personality. The upside of this process is the opportunity to create any client she wants.

For the 2016 San Francisco Decorator Showcase, her imaginary clients were rocker David Bowie and his iconic wife, Iman. The showcase took place a year after David Bowie died, turning the effort into a tribute of sorts. After his passing, Tineke read about the couple's long-term love affair, which was clearly rich with meaning and profoundly committed but also quite private. She imagined how they might have spent their lives in private, which led to the room "David and Iman."

The 2016 showcase house was set in a 1930s home on the top of Telegraph Hill, with sweeping views of the bay. Tineke was tapped to design the primary bedroom, a double-sized room set on the home's top floor with wide views of the city and the bay. The room's size allowed for a sleeping area, seating area, and small writing area. Influenced by the views of the water and fog, she designed a room for the pair in serene hues of blue and gray, with an abundance of texture. Arresting artwork and hits of black give the room an appropriate rocker edge.

Above: In the bathroom, geometric lines play to the masculine, while the organic forms in the engineered stone countertops are musical in their movement. **Opposite:** The large master suite allowed Tineke to carve out a small writing space, defined by a Baker console and dining chair and styled to perfection.

EN VOGUE
SALON

In 2015, the San Francisco Decorator Showcase house was set in a Julia Morgan–design Tudor mansion in the city's Pacific Heights neighborhood. Tasked with designing the master bath within a space graced with high ceilings and beautiful crown moldings, Tineke chose to tell the story of high fashion. More accurately, she decided to tell her interpretation of that story.

Taking her inspiration from an iconic Vogue cover from 1960, Tineke designed a room equally fashion-forward and whimsical and more than a little daring. Overlooking the scene, and defining the space, is a photograph reinterpreting the cover pose. Ever fearless, Tineke posed for the photo herself.

Rendered primarily in black and white with the drama of a runway debut, the room is a study in confident contrasts. The crisp black-and-white room is accented with a regal emerald green sofa and crowned by a Zia Priven chandelier that pointedly hangs just above the portrait, seeming to crown its subject. Copious gilded accents are high-style and high-impact, especially when paired with a lavatory dressed in graffiti by artist Elan Evans of Elan Atelier. A soft, cloud-like pattern painted in gold on the ceiling—also by Elan Evans—balances the solid geometric patterns on the floor and in the artwork. The small dressing room, envisioned as a place to put on makeup and jewelry, is covered in a collage of black-and-white Vogue covers.

Mixing high and low, elegant and edgy, well-known pieces with custom-created objects and flights of fancy are Tineke's hallmarks. Most of all, every Tineke Triggs design tells a story, and this room is no exception.

Previous overleaf: A Palermo light fixture from Zia Priven quite literally crowns the room, hanging just above a portrait of Tineke—a recreation of an iconic *Vogue* cover photographed in 1964 by Irving Penn. **Above:** Graffiti artwork by Elan Evans in the lavatory is designed to inspire confidence with abstractions of the words "joy," "strength," "love," and "forgiveness." **Right:** Custom mirrors flanking the original oval window above the vanity— custom designed with GO Build Studio and built by Cook Construction—are perfectly integrated into the existing molding.

Above: Tineke envisioned the small dressing room as a place to put on makeup and jewelry. The lighting fixtures—Ice Glass by J.T. Kalmar and Celestial Pebble by OCHRE—act as jewelry for the room. "To me, the pendants feel like luxurious earrings," says Tineke. **Opposite:** Tineke double-backed a vinyl fabric—a collage of black-and-white *Vogue* covers from James Malone—with acrylic to use as wallpaper.

LIQUID LOUNGE

Created for the 2020 San Francisco Decorator Showcase, the Liquid Lounge, and Cala Mezcal Tequila Bar are the stuff of fantasy. Set in the lower regions of a 6,500-square-foot home built in 1926 in the tony Outer Richmond neighborhood of West Clay Park, this multipurpose room is a party destination, pure and simple. Due to the COVID-19 pandemic, the forty-third annual showcase was virtual, making this particular set of party rooms a much-needed fantasy for many.

Tineke's goal was to design a joy-filled retreat, envisioning it as a hangout for a young, fun-loving couple. A dynamic, interactive, entertaining space, it goes far beyond the expected. An amalgam of postmodern, Memphis, and pop art influences, the design incorporates the unconventional patterns, abstract decoration, and asymmetrical design of the Memphis movement, colors and shapes of Postmodern design, and references to supergraphics from the 1970s.

In the Liquid Lounge, kinetic artworks by Ryan Bucko and Liquid Canvas face one another across the highly experiential space colored in ochre, rose gold, and black. The Liquid Canvas work was the first of its kind—a hand-animated sequence based on a painting by Bay Area artist Lauren McIntosh that brings the static image to life.

True to form, no corner is overlooked. Stylized chairs—each with its own character—pull up to a game table. Custom bookshelves with brass rod details deftly incorporate the lower floors' high windows, and a lowered acoustic ceiling is given new life with a supergraphic-like pattern. Rather than cover up awkward level changes that resemble stadium seating, Tineke leaned in, turning them into a DJ station complete with a custom-made acrylic shelf for the vintage turntable.

Behind the rose gold curtain, the Cala Tequila Bar feels like a private club. Here, Tineke lets loose her love for tequila and for Mexico. On the walls, she commissioned a moody, ethereal painting of the mountains of Baha. Metal paneling by Artefactura tucked behind an IPE screen is dramatically backlit. A snake slithers across the table. Above the sofa, Daniel Canogar's "Amalgama" uses an algorithm to liquefy famous historical works of art in a pattern that, mesmerizingly, never repeats.

Here, it's always five o'clock.

Previous overleaf: At the game table, mismatched chairs take on a life of their own and, at a glance, could be mistaken for people sitting down for a game of chess. The Skyline Chess Set is one of Tineke's favorites.

Top left: The three-dimensional artwork "Linear Interplay" by Ryan Bunko hangs above the sofa.

Left: A custom sectional from Arden Home wraps the corner, while a geometric table from Birnam Wood Studio defies gravity.

Opposite: Golden hues and abstract geometric shapes dominate the lively, interactive lounge. A golden-hued custom rug from Scott Group Studio is the "yellow brick road" that draws visitors into the seating area. Above the Jean de Merry sideboard, an oil painting by Bay Area artist Lauren McIntosh is reinterpreted in video by Liquid Canvas, subtly moving and changing over time.

Opposite: In this retreat within a retreat, a custom bar wall by Pellandini & Co. is backed by a wall system by ARTEFACTcurator set into the slatted-wood wall. Catenary Bar Stools from Token pull up to a snake-topped table from GO Build Studio. "After the last few years, I think everyone needs a bar in their house," says Tineke. **Above:** The sweeping curves of the raspberry-hued banquette by Arden Home, white origami forms of the Stephen Antonson table, and kinetic artwork by Daniel Canogar positively pop against the bar's moody mural by Caroline Lizarraga.

PROJECT TEAMS

CITY LIVING

BOLD AND BALANCED
Art consultant: SB Fine Arts
Contractor: Cook Construction
Landscape: Terra Ferma Landscapes
Photographer: R. Brad Knipstein

BEAUTY AND THE BEAST
Architect: Ari Gessler Architects
Contractor: Aaron Gordon
Photographer: Drew Kelly

FASHION FORWARD
Photographer: Christopher Stark
Photo Stylist: Yedda Morrison

TEXTURAL TREASURES
Art consultant: Alexandra Ray Art
  Advisory
Contractor: Jeff King & Company
Photographer: Paul Dyer

URBAN ECLECTIC
Architect: Hood Thomas Architects
Contractor: Red Horse Construction
Landscape Architect: Alexis Donohue
Art Consultant: Alice Ranahan Art
  Advisory
Photographer: Aubrie Pick
Photo Stylist: Allegra Hsiao

GREEN WITH ENVY
Contractor: Heirloom Builders
Photographer: Christopher Stark
Photo Stylist: Allegra Hsiao

FURTHER AFIELD

ALL ABOUT MARILYN
Contractor: Cook Construction
Landscape Architect: Stephanie
  Green
Photographer: Christopher Stark

TRADITIONAL TWIST
Architect: Nyhus Design Group
Contractor: Colindres & Associates
Photographer: John Merkl

MAVERICK ROMANCE
Architect: TRG Architecture & Interior
  Design
Contractor: K Welton Construction
Landscape Architect: Michael Callan
Photographer: R. Brad Knipstein
Photo Stylist: Mikhael Romain

BAYFRONT DEBONAIRE
Photographer: Jose Manuel Alorda

GLAM GETAWAYS

MOUNTAIN MODERN
Architect: Walton Architecture &
  Engineering
Art Consultant: Zener Schon
  Contemporary Art
Contractor: Vineyard Custom Homes
Photographer: Philip Harvey

CAMP GETAWAY
Architect: Ryan Group Architects
Contractor: Crestwood Construction
Photographer: R. Brad Knipstein

A PLACE TO PLAY
Architect: Stacey Ford
Contractor: George T. Flynn
Landscape Architect: Stephanie
  Green
Photographer: Suzanna Scott

SURF SCENE
Architect: Moller Architecture
Contractor: Woodworking West
Landscape Architect: Terra Ferma
  Landscapes
Photographer: R. Brad Knipstein
Accessories Stylist: Cyia Batten

PARTY WAVE
Contractor: John Fuchs Construction
Photographer: R. Brad Knipstein

COASTAL CABANA
Photographer: Paul Dyer
Photo Stylist: Pattee Stayrook

SHOWCASE HOMES

LIQUID LOUNGE
Contractor: John Pellandini &
 Company
Decorative Painter: Caroline Lizarraga
 and Elan Evans
Photographer: Christopher Stark

DAVID AND IMAN
Photographer: Christopher Stark

EN VOGUE SALON
Photographer: Eric Rorer

PORTRAITS

TINEKE TRIGGS
Kimberly M. Wang

CHASE REYNOLDS EWALD &
HEATHER HEBERT
Pamela Casaudoumecq

ABOUT THE AUTHORS

INSPIRED BY DESIGNERS WHO BROKE AWAY FROM THE PACK, Tineke is known for creating soulful, artistic and imaginative interiors. By mastering both the art and science of design, her work gives rise to a unique form of design mixology. Her elevated interiors not only provoke the senses, but deliver on the details that create truly memorable spaces.

The veteran of six San Francisco Decorator Showcases, her award-winning work has been featured in numerous publications including *Architectural Digest, Elle Decor, Veranda, Dwell, Luxe, California Home & Design, Modern Luxury Interiors, California Homes* and *Sunset Magazine.*

When not designing, Tineke enjoys working on her tennis game, kickboxing, family time on the beach, and traveling down the coast with her vintage 1973 Airstream in tow. Tineke lives in San Francisco with her husband, Will, and their two teenage sons.

CHASE REYNOLDS EWALD'S CAREER INCLUDES MORE THAN 15 books, 2 Western Design Conference Sourcebooks, and hundreds of magazine articles. A graduate of Yale and U.C. Berkeley's Graduate School of Journalism, Chase is a freelance writer, editor and book packager who helps clients craft their stories. Recent titles include *Cabin Style, American Rustic, Modern Americana,* the multi-award-winning *Bison: Portrait of an Icon,* and, with Heather Sandy Hebert, *At Home in the Wine Country.* She lives in northern California with her husband and four daughters.

AS THE DAUGHTER OF A TALENTED ARCHITECT, HEATHER Sandy Hebert has spent a lifetime immersed in the fields of architecture and design. A graduate of U.C. Berkeley and the University of San Francisco Graduate School of Business, she spent over 25 years directing marketing and communications for an international architecture practice before leaving to found her own consulting practice and dedicate her time to writing about design. She now works with design professionals to help them tell their stories and achieve their design and business goals, and contributes to a number of design publications. Her first book, *The New Architecture of Wine,* was published in 2019 and her second book, *At Home in the Wine Country,* written with Chase Reynolds Ewald, was released in 2021.

ACKNOWLEDGMENTS

Good design starts with a vision, but it takes a team to make it happen.

I couldn't do what I do—and this book would not exist—without the best clients in the world, so many of whom have become close friends; my fantastic coworkers at Tineke Triggs Interiors; my collaborators, a talented group of builders, architects, and artisans; and the most loyal support system of family and friends anyone could ask for. They're my tribe.

To my clients: You are the reason I do what I do. I literally couldn't do it without you. Thank you to each and every one of you for believing in me, trusting me, and giving me the freedom to not hold back.

To my team: I can't thank you enough. You are tireless and positive, and you make this company better!

To Julie: You are the perfect complement to my craft—always have been, always will be.

To the BGs: You are my sisters for life!

Working on this book has been the culmination of a dream. Kudos to the team that made it happen: Tama, my right-hand taskmaster and can-do companion; Chase and Heather, talented writers and new friends who gave voice to my work and made the process fun; and our team at Gibbs Smith. Our editor Juree Sondker, copy and production editor Sue Collier, and book designers Ryan Thomann and Virginia Snow brought this book to life, and I can't thank them enough.

In every project, I like to leave a symbol of a dragonfly somewhere in the house. For many centuries, dragonflies have been a symbol of happiness, new beginnings, and change. The dragonfly means hope, change, and love—it's a symbol of all that I hope to imbue in each home I have the privilege of designing.

To Will, for always believing in me and for providing unending faith, support, and love, and to my boys, who make me work harder and give me purpose. —TT

First Edition
27 26 25 24 23   5 4 3 2 1

Text © 2023 Tineke Triggs, Chase Reynolds Ewald, and Heather Sandy Hebert

Photographs © 2023 **Jose Manuel Alorda** 136–45; **Wichai Bopatay/EyeEm via Getty Images** endsheets; **Pamela Casaudoumecq** 238 bottom; **Paul Dyer** 38–49, 146–47, 204–15; **Philip Harvey** 148–57; **Drew Kelly** 2–3, 14–25; **R. Brad Knipstein** 4, 11, 26–37, 88–9, 120–35, 158–69, 182–93, 194–203, 237; **John Merkl** 106–19; **Aubrie Pick** 12–13, 50–61; **Eric Rorer** 6, 224–29; **Suzanna Scott** 170–81; **Christopher Stark** 1, 62–77, 78–87, 90–105, 230–35, 216–17, 219–23; **Kimberly M. Wang** 8, 238 top

Published by
Gibbs Smith
P.O. Box 667
Layton, Utah 84041

1.800.835.4993 orders
www.gibbs-smith.com

Designer: Virginia Snow
Art director: Ryan Thomann
Editor: Juree Sondker
Production editor: Sue Collier
Production manager: Felix Gregario

Printed and bound in China

Gibbs Smith books are printed on either recycled, 100% post-consumer waste, FSC-certified papers or on paper produced from sustainable PEFC-certified forest/controlled wood source. Learn more at www.pefc.org.

Library of Congress Control Number: 2023935674

ISBN: 978-1-4236-6368-3